BRUMROAMIN
BIRMINGHAM AND MIDLAND
ROMANY GYPSY AND TRAVELLER CULTURE

BRUMROAMIN
BIRMINGHAM AND MIDLAND
ROMANY GYPSY AND TRAVELLER CULTURE

By Ted Rudge

I dedicate this book with heartfelt gratitude to my wife Maureen for the encouragement, support and loyalty given to everything that I have achieved.

Brumroamin - Birmingham and Midland Romany Gypsy and Traveller Culture
Copyright © 2003 Ted Rudge.

The rights of Ted Rudge to be identified as authors of this work have been asserted by them in accordance with the Copyright, Design and Patents Act 1988.

CIP catalogue record for this book is available from the British Library.

ISBN: 0709302460

Published by Birmingham Library and Information Services.

Designed and produced by Birmingham City Council.

Front: Travelling Showman's living van © Henry Roper

Back: The Author at the Black Patch © Ted Rudge

CONTENTS

FOREWORD

Birmingham has one great natural resource - its people. Unlike most other great centres of population, the city cannot boast anything remarkable in its physical features. Sited as it is almost as far from the sea as is possible in England, it has been unable to benefit from the advantages of having a port or docks such as those which helped to propel London, Cardiff, Glasgow and Dublin onto the world stage. Nor is Birmingham at the crossing point of a major river. It has watercourses; the River Rea especially has played a part in the making of Brum. But like the Rivers Cole and Tame, the Rea is short in length, shallow in depth and narrow in width. It was navigable only by tiny pleasure boats and its main purpose was as a source of drinking water and of power for mills.

Bereft of a major river and far from the sea, Birmingham was also unable to boast of its status as a defensive position. It has no impressive crag as does Edinburgh, nor can it declare that it possesses a steep hill as does Dudley. It has no castle - although Weoley Castle recalls a fortified manor house - and its lords were minor players on the regional and national stage. Finally, Birmingham cannot even claim to have been blessed by abundance of resources beneath the ground. Its major physical feature is its red sandstone which has been used in constructing its buildings, but Birmingham has not been able to profit from the presence of coal, iron, limestone or fire clay as have so many other places.

Birmingham is a product of the skills, talents, ingenuity, adaptability and inventiveness of its own people. The recognition of this reality has led to a growth in interest in the peoples of Brum. Family and local historians have stressed the importance of English migrants from Warwickshire, Worcestershire and Staffordshire in the transformation of Birmingham from a lowly agricultural hamlet into a renowned manufacturing centre; other historians have drawn attention to the significance of the Welsh, the Scots, the Irish and the Italians in pushing Brum forward into its status as The City of A Thousand Trades; and increasingly, research is shifting towards emphasising the contribution made by Black and South Asian Brummies in leading Birmingham on the way to becoming a paradigm for multi-cultural Britain.

Despite these studies, many gaps in our knowledge remain to be filled. We need to know more about the Yemenis of Brum, the Germans, the Chinese and others and there are those who are determined to attend to the histories of these peoples. For all the good and crucial work which has been and is being carried out, one of the peoples of Birmingham has failed to attract more than cursory notice - that is, until now. They are the Romanies. With his history of the Black Patch Romanies, Ted Rudge has ensured that these people will not be forgotten. They will be recalled and so too will their contribution to Birmingham's history. Ted has done something to which all historians should aspire. He has shed light on a people who have been hidden from view. He has pulled the Romanies into the gaze of history and in so doing he has ensured that we take note of them and appreciate them. Ted's study is a pioneering one and it is to be hoped that others will follow in his trail so that the history of the Romanies of Nechells and elsewhere in Brum can also be brought to the fore. On Our Dad's side, I have two great-great-grandmothers who were Romanies. With Romany blood in me but with little knowledge of my Romany forebears, I pay tribute to Ted Rudge and the job he has done in enlightening me and others.

(Professor Carl Chinn MBE)

INTRODUCTION

In the Romany language the word that describes a non-gypsy is *'gaujo'*. I am a gaujo who has had the privilege of researching the social history of a community of tent and *'vardo'* (caravan) dwellers who lived in the Midlands from the mid-nineteenth to the early twentieth century. The area they chose to live in was known as the 'Black Patch'. Why this group settled on this particular camping ground and how they eventually became integrated with families of gaujos in three neighbouring districts is recorded here for the first time.

Initial research into this subject formed the final part of my Certificate of Higher Education in Birmingham Studies at Birmingham University during 1999 and 2000. I started this course five years after retiring from British Telecom (BT) with whom I spent all of my working life. I was born and lived the first twenty years of my life in Winson Green, one of the areas explored in this book.

Additional investigative research for my course work included making contact with many descendants and neighbours of the original group of Black Patch settlers. They told me stories that have been passed down orally through their families and neighbours over the last one hundred and fifty years. They generally thought that this could be the last opportunity of capturing their stories before they were forgotten forever. Unfortunately, no evidence could be found of any contemporary gypsy material published by or about this, mostly, illiterate group during the nineteenth century. However, newspaper articles published in the early 1900s and some from the 1950s, together with official reports and the stories from their families, have provided the source material for this book.

Definitions of what constitutes a genuine gypsy are fraught with difficulty given the history of intermarriage between gypsies and settled people as well as other travelling groups. To avoid becoming embroiled in complex arguments I have accepted and recorded the assertions of my interviewees and other sources.

People from many countries, of different colours, creeds and cultures today inhabit Birmingham and its surrounding area. This was not the case a hundred and fifty years ago when gypsies were able to roam the countryside living the same lifestyle their ancestors had led many centuries before. Country pursuits were then a way of life of which the gypsy community was a part. Heath and farming land were key features of the local geography, but this pattern of life was about to change forever, for both the gypsies and their neighbours.

Gypsies are a race of people who have always known persecution but who have managed to find a way of adapting and moving on, often baffling their persecutors in the process. When the Black Patch Romany Gypsies could no longer hold on to their *'gypsyrie'* (urban camping ground), the way of life for the majority changed irrevocably.

CHAPTER ONE
WHERE DID THEY COME FROM?

M Before any story about gypsies can be told, some understanding of the dark-haired, dark-eyed and dark-skinned race of people who eventually were given this name is necessary. Modern perceptions of the gypsy are somewhat confused; the names 'Tinker' or 'New Age Traveller' have been inaccurately substituted. Gypsies have a culture which is over a thousand years old, together with a proud tradition and the ability to speak at least two languages; their own and the tongue of their country of settlement. Today, an estimated eight to twelve million gypsies are integrated with the populations of many countries across the world, with no single country being their own. How did it all begin? This question has occupied the thoughts of many historians; the following is a brief account of some popular answers and theories passed down to descendants of the gypsies and retold to me.

In approximately 1000AD a large group of people migrated from northwest India. This could have been due to military action, religious persecution, slavery or simply an already nomadic group venturing further afield. Historians base their claims on several words found in the Romany language that are common to northwest India. There were seven tent-dwelling tribes who moved around like Bedouins, originally living in northern India. They made a living by storytelling and some had the ability to tell fortunes. They eventually left their homes to escape some kind of tyranny which had befallen them at this time.

Their migration took a westward route from India and, on the way, sections of the groups settled in the countries through which they passed. When they reached Egypt, they encountered the bright, colourful silks which they incorporated into their clothing. They also took up belly dancing, and the use of biblical names. Some gypsies made their way to Russia, where the Cossack influence was absorbed, gaining their love and understanding of horsemanship. They also developed their passion for dance at this stage. Transylvania, where modern books and films generally depict gypsies sitting around a campfire, was also visited. Some musical skills were gained in Hungary, especially the playing of the violin which led to the development of gypsy violin orchestras. On arrival in Romania they adopted the name Romany. Most of their travelling until now had been done on foot. However, at this point proper road systems were encountered for the first time, facilitating wheeled travel. Primitive wagons eventually became the preferred mode of transport making their journeys much faster. As unwanted strangers in many countries, the gypsies often adopted the guise of pilgrims, and sometimes they were even granted letters of safe passage. Before Spain temporarily exiled the gypsies, flamenco dance was absorbed into their culture. Knowledge of Egyptian silks, reinforced by the colourful flowing dress needed for flamenco, enhanced the entertainment appeal of the gypsy. On their initial arrival in Europe these dark-skinned, colourfully dressed travelling people were mistaken for Egyptians and a derivative of this word led eventually to the name now given to this group - gypsy. The need for self-preservation during the journey helped nurture their secretive nature causing the people of host countries to be suspicious of them. Their self-sufficiency engendered transportable skills, such as horse-dealing, dancing, living off the land, herbal cures, fortune-telling and wood and metalworking. Woodworking skills were common amongst the Black Forest gypsies before their eviction from Germany in 1500. France followed the German example by banishing gypsies shortly afterwards.

Studies of the Romany Gypsy language have revealed words that are only found in certain other languages enabling historians to plot the routes taken by the early gypsies. Despite the legislative evictions that were imposed on gypsies during the fifteenth and sixteenth centuries in various countries where they settled, some gypsy groups must have covertly integrated into society. Today gypsies can be found throughout the world, having flourished in some countries more than in others.

CHAPTER TWO
ARRIVAL AND SURVIVAL IN ENGLAND

 The first recorded incidence of gypsy travellers reaching the shores of the British Isles was in 1505. Quotes relating to their arrival and subsequent movements can be found in the *Journal of the Gypsy Lore Society*, Vol 1, p 7. In July 1505 King James IV of Scotland wrote to the King of Denmark:

Anthony Gagino, a lord of Little Egypt, who, with his retinue, had a few months previously reached Scotland during a pilgrimage through the Christian world, undertaken at the command of the Apostolic

The gypsies who arrived eventually divided and travelled the length of Scotland, England, Wales and Ireland. The following is an extract from a coroner's inquest in 1514:

One of the witnesses mentioned an Egyptian woman who had been lodging in Lambeth....and who could tell marvellous things by looking into one's hand.

confirming that within nine years, gypsies had reached London.

An Act of Parliament, the Egyptians Act of 1530, was passed twenty-five years after the Egyptians (gypsies) first arrived. Its main purpose was to prevent any further immigration from the continent of Europe and to expel those that were already in the country. A grim reinforcement of the Act came into being in 1554 and remained on the statute books for the next two hundred years, declaring that any gypsy found in England could be put to death. What had the travellers done to warrant such legislation? It may have been the

country's fear of Catholicism or a general dislike of anything foreign. Where would they have gone had they obeyed the Act? How did they manage to survive and prosper? The answers are beyond the scope of this book but it is sufficient to say that during this period many gypsies did evade the death sentence and continued living in traditional ways. The Act was repealed in 1783 following the introduction of several legislative measures relating to rogues, vagabonds and sturdy beggars. At the Devonshire Lent Assizes of 1598 Charles, Oliver and Bartholomew Baptist were charged with 'wandering like Egyptians'. *Journal of the Gypsy Lore Society*, Vol 1, p 23)

At the Quarter Sessions held in Richmond, Yorkshire, in 1605, a Robert Metcalf was brought before the Grand Jury for harbouring 'in his dwelling house five men and boys, being gypsies...for four days and nights together to the great terror of his neighbours'.

State Papers of 31 January 1613 reveal 'some Egyptians [gypsies] in Leicestershire refusing to disband when summoned, the Earl of Huntingdon sent forces against them, which led to a report that Papists were arming'. Clearly, legislation that had been put in place with the intention of ridding England of gypsies had not worked.

The following baptismal record of a Midland traveller can be found in the register of Aston Parish Church (St Peter and St Paul) dated 12 May 1591. Circumstances relating to the entry may never be known, but the contrasting entries for that day underline the social differences that existed.

Marr.	{ John Turner { Ann Bucknall	...	...	...	...	...	3 May
Bap.	Henry fil Martin Day		...	...	...	... 10	„
Bur.	Joane Fallowes, Weeddowe			...	...	... 12	„
Bap.	"Henry Reade the sonn of Henry Reade of Aston was baptized the xxııth day of May beinge Whitsunday even. Henry Williams Vicar of Aston & Henry Cooke godfatheer"						
„	"A bastard out of Yerdington was baptized a trauellinge woman brought a bedd in the streete. Hard harted people"						

Baptism entry in the register of Aston Parish Church 1591

By the eighteenth century, England had gypsies in every county, who travelled the countryside during the summer months, covering approximately seven to ten miles a day, and stopping to work on the land for as long as employment was available. Working trails soon developed, resulting in the establishment of more or less fixed routes for each gypsy group. The length of the routes depended on the geography of an area and, as gypsies did not like winter travel, they always returned to their base to overwinter, often near one of the large industrial cities. Alternatively, a town or village was chosen where they camped on unused land near to a source of water. It was from these winter quarters that horse-dealing, trotting races and bare-knuckle fights were arranged and handmade items like clothes pegs, flowers, meat skewers and other trinkets were produced. What small amount of education the gypsy child received would have been obtained during the winter months because in the summer children were just another pair of working hands. Literacy rates among the gypsies have always been low in comparison with those of the settled population, on whom gypsies often relied to read documents for them. Illiteracy was overcome by relaying any important events of the past or present orally but, as in most oral traditions, parts were omitted or elaborated upon.

CHAPTER THREE
TYPES OF TRAVELLERS

A Travelling Showman's living van. Louise Roper, the mother, helped out at any birth that occurred at the fairground, acting as an unofficial fairground midwife. Her own children Dolly, Harry and the youngest Sidney are seen with her overwintering in a yard in Beales Street, Aston near the Serpentine ground (Henry Roper) 1917

The title 'gypsy' loosely defines a person belonging to a family of travelling people. Within this broad grouping, other travelling groups have their own identifying title just like the Romany. One late-twentieth century travelling group that is very distinct from the gypsy (but often referred to as such) are New Age travellers who live a communal open-air life in groups and travel around in motor vehicles. They embody a free-spirited lifestyle, attending the Summer Solstice and other pagan festivals but their unconventional lifestyle often conflicts with views held by the settled population. Another group often incorrectly referred to as gypsies are fairground people. This assumption may stem from the similarity of their lifestyles. Both travel during the summer and overwinter in large units, living in their chosen mode of transport. Additionally gypsies often have a presence at fairgrounds where they make money from fortune-telling, boxing, horse-trading or simply helping to erect the fairground. John Loveridge tells of his granddad Leonard and his father Bert (nicknamed Maize):

Granddad had several horses which he kept on some common land in Handsworth New Road., Pat Collins' fair was held there once a year, granddad's family ran a Boxing Booth inviting all comers to 'fist cuff' fight 'Bare Knuckles'. This was the life of the gypsies, horses and fighting to live. In his youth dad had to be very hard always having to fight. My granddad used to fight even when he was 70. Dad was always sorting things out for him.

Bert (Maize) Loveridge, son of Leonard c1960 (Loveridge family)

Pugilism was popular with gypsies. Fred Badger tells how his gypsy brothers, Edward (Teddy) and Thomas (Tommy), were never frightened of a challenge especially if it involved making money. For many years in the middle of the twentieth century a travelling fair visited waste ground at the junction of Boulton Road and Handsworth New Road where offers to fight bare-fisted were made to the local lads. The challenge involved trying to last three rounds with seasoned fighters and if you managed to stay on your feet the reward was £3. Either Teddy or Tommy would consistently bring the prize money home, proudly handing it over to their mom. They only kept the broken nose! What the opposition probably did not know was that both the brothers were in the fight game. Teddy eventually became the head trainer for the Royal Mint Amateur Boxing Club in Icknield Street, Hockley.

Terry Wallace from Erdington is a direct descendant of fairground people called Shepherd. Shepherd's Travelling Fair was established in the early 1800s and was eventually sold to the Walsall-based Pat Collins Fun Fair. Terry's family have 'Showman' as their occupation on their official documents, whilst gypsies are often classified as Hawker, Pedlar, Chimney Sweep, Labourer or even Umbrella Repairer. Terry's mother, Florrie, and her sister, Elsie, (both Shepherds) were born just after the outbreak of the First World War and both were raised on a fairground circuit, travelling annually throughout the Black Country and Birmingham. The Onion Fair at Aston and Handsworth Flower Show were among the many stops made before travelling on as far as Nottingham Races. At first their parents could not afford a wagon and found lodgings wherever the fair was pitched. The education received by the sisters was fragmented as they attended a local school only for the duration of the fair at the insistence of a School Board officer, following his visit to the fairground people. Eventually both sisters married 'flatties', the fairground term for non-fairground workers.

In the early 1970s teachers at the Rushey-Mead School in Leicester were informed of the arrival of the usual winter intake of children following the annual Nottingham Goose Fair. One new teacher, Celia Scottow, anticipated their imminent arrival with apprehension. Celia was pleasantly surprised when the new intake arrived well-dressed, clean and extremely polite and, although way behind with their education, very keen to learn.

Non-gypsy children, when playing, would often unwittingly use a disparaging song that has been passed down through the generations:

My mother said I never should,
Play with the gypsies in the wood.
If I did, she would say,
Naughty girl to disobey.
Disobey, disobey,
Naughty girl to disobey.

Bender tent in use 2003

Gypsy children were taunted by non-gypsy children with:

Gypsy, gypsy lives in a tent,
Because your mom can't pay the rent.

David Badger recalls:

In my street and school I used to be called 'gypo' because of my black greasy looking hair and because of this I had many a fight with the local lads from Summer Lane.

"Gypo' is one of the derogatory names often used insultingly to describe travelling people by non-travellers who also frequently associate incorrectly the term 'tinker' in the same disparaging way. However tinkers, now commonly known as 'travellers', whose origin is thought to have come from a group of wandering poets and scholars, were eventually joined by other Irish people forced to vacate their land during times of social and economic upheaval such as the Great Famine. Despite many centuries of co-existing with gypsies in England, ultimately resulting in some cultural exchange and intermarriage, the traveller remains a distinct ethnic group. They have their own secret language 'Shelta', also known as 'Gammon' or 'Cant'. The word tinker refers to their original transportable skill of metalworking derived from the Irish word 'ceard' (smith), so 'tinceard'

(tinsmith). They would mend or sell household utensils like tin pots, pans and buckets as they travelled. These traditional crafts have been superseded by more modern ways of earning money due to urbanisation and the introduction of products made from plastic. Irish travellers are still an, often controversial, feature of urban life in the Midlands and their story deserves its own book.

From the eighteenth century the newly-built canal networks of England led to a new and more efficient system for transporting goods and with it a new type of gypsy. Whole families known as 'water gypsies' were reared on the working barges, as the families travelled the canals carrying goods such as coal, used in homes as well as in industry. Water gypsies had winter stops like their land-based counterparts, but their 'rests' were enforced due to frozen canals. When this happened their earnings ceased until they were able to move again. A story often told by descendants of water gypsies involved transporting coal from A to B and making extra cash for a rainy day. In order to make the trip faster, some coal was surreptitiously removed from the barge and either sold or dumped in the canal. Before the weight of the barge could be checked by measuring the waterline at the delivery end, water was added to the coal to make up the missing weight.

Albert Smart (1912-1999) was one of twelve children in a water gypsy family. They worked the canals between Liverpool and Birmingham transporting coal or pottery, and eventually built up a business owning more than three working barges plus a livery stable in Great Barr Street, Birmingham. Albert's early water gypsy life was hard. As part of a large family living in the restricted space of the barge, the children had to sleep on top of the cargo with only their coats for a bed. To prevent the younger children from falling overboard they were tied to the barge with a rope, but this did not always prevent a drowning. Feeding was a major task normally performed as the barge was in motion. Alternatively the children would line up on the side of the canal to receive what was available which was often only bread and 'scrape' (dripping). When frozen canals prevented the movement of the barges, these enforced stops afforded one advantage - a limited opportunity for education. Local schools would (reluctantly) accept the water gypsy children into their classrooms. During their short stay the gypsy children were ostracized, not by other children, but by the teachers. As soon as the canal water thawed their education stopped, resulting in low education levels. Albert always said: 'As long as you could sign your name that's all the education you needs'.

Albert's life as a water gypsy changed after he married a Romany gypsy girl. His wife had led a traditional travelling lifestyle with her family, the Romany Drapers and Boswells. Starting in the Cotswolds at the end of each winter, the Romany route took them as far as Somerset before returning to the Cotswolds for the winter. Whether she could not live on a barge or he in a caravan is not clear, but after 1939 they settled in a brick built house and raised a family. One of their daughters, Victoria, although now living in a Birmingham suburb, retains Romany traditions. The interior of her house resembles a gypsy caravan with plates and dinner services displayed on the walls together with pictures of the gypsy lifestyle. She was married in the gypsy tradition in Somerset by jumping the broomstick then crossing fire and water followed by a civil ceremony to legitimise the marriage. Victoria (known as Toria) and her partner often visit gypsy gatherings both locally and around the country.

Victoria (Toria) and partner's wedding jumping the fire (Toria Pownall)

A new group of gypsies began to arrive in Birmingham in recent years. This has resulted from social, political and economic upheaval in their native countries in Eastern Europe. It is too early to predict how they will fare in their adopted home.

CHAPTER FOUR
CULTURE

Jessie Loveridge now and aged 17

 Jessie Loveridge recalls being raised by parents who were once part of the travelling culture and has brought to mind the hardship endured as a child. The Romany ways have never left Jessie and still mean a great deal to her:

Sara May, my mother, (1888-1940) was always known as May, she took in washing to earn a few more coppers; on Mondays she lit the brew house fire at six in the morning and was waiting for the pawnshop in Foundry Lane to open at nine. My father, Leonard, (c1870-1940) always seemed poorly to me, he was one of the Romany gypsies evicted from the Black Patch. On Sundays I had to

visit my Aunty Byna who lived in Avery Road. We were told she was the Queen of the gypsies. One day I cut my foot very badly, dad wrapped the cut with fatty bacon and cloth and it completely healed the cut, sixty five years later I had a cancerous spot removed from my leg but it would not heal, I did what dad had done all those years ago and it very soon healed.

Today I live a quiet life; my door is always open, as I cannot be closed in. Gypsy instincts have led me to live in 15 different homes and I am not finished yet. As my dad always did, I still would not go out without wearing a red neckerchief around my neck.

Leonard Loveridge aged 70 c1930 (Loveridge family)

Bright coloured clothing worn by the gypsies often included the colour red.

Lois Pearson remembers her friend Gerty Loveridge's father was a tall dark-haired man who always wore a spotted red handkerchief tied around his neck and was very strict with his children.

Esau, King of the Black Patch gypsies, was described by journalist Ellery Jephcott as:

Dressed in the characteristic knee breeches, velvet coat adorned with immense pearl buttons and made with capacious 'poachers pockets' double breasted brightly coloured waistcoat, and thick boots...

George Owen remembered that his father Edward earned the nickname of Teddy-Odden

because he once sold a pair of shoes to an Irish navvy on the cut (canal) knowing them to be both left feet. Retribution followed in the Gate pub on Booth Street, Handsworth, where Teddy-Odden finished up through the window, landing in the street. In the same pub, one of the corners of the bowling green was known as Owen's Corner in his memory.

Edward Owen 1883-1923 c1900 (Irene Lane)

Drink was also responsible for the following appearance at Smethwick Magistrates Court, which was reported in the *Smethwick Telephone* in 1900:

A serious fracas among the gypsies of the 'Black Patch' on May 21st resulted in Mary Ann Scarrett (35), married woman, who occupied a van on this notorious spot, being charged with unlawfully wounding an old woman named Sarah Davies.

The complainant, who appeared in the witness box with her head swathed in bandages, said that although she was not married, she was the mother of 18 children. On the date in question she met the prisoner as she was leaving a public house in the vicinity and a quarrel ensued. The prisoner said the complainant was just the woman she wanted to meet and struck her a blow with a jug, exclaiming, 'I was about to fetch milk, but I will fetch blood'... The bench reduced the charge to one of assault, and for the defence Mr Glover contended that the complainant was the aggressor, and the parties had a 'fair fight' the complainant received her injuries through falling down. A fine of 10s plus costs (in all £2 0s 6d) was imposed, in default, 14 days imprisonment.

Ken Loveridge confirms that:

The Romanies had little or no education, but were brilliant musicians playing by ear. They busked in clubs and pubs with their concertinas and violins, string, and wind instruments.

George Owen wrote songs and poems and loved to sing himself. George suddenly passed away in early January 2001 and, after George's funeral, his family found his written work. The following piece is in his memory:

George Cyril Owen (Linda Farley)

MY VALLEY OF LOVE

*When my name is called up yonder
And I leave this world behind
Another land I'll try to find
I know it's in the heavens above
When I find it I shall call it
My valley of love*

*In my valley of love
The sun shines every day
No rain nor any snow
The cold winds never blow
That's my valley of love*

*Now my valley of love
Is in the heavens above
It's quite easy to find
If you want peace of mind
With angel's harps a-playing
You're welcome anytime
In my valley of love*

*In my valley of love
There's laughter everywhere
Songbirds fill the air
It's roses, roses all the way
And if you should pass any day
You're welcome anytime to stay
In my valley of love*

*In my valley of love
There's no darkness no strife
Only everlasting life
If it's happiness you need
No matter your colour or creed
You're welcome anytime
In my valley of love*

Jessie Loveridge recollects:

'Neither dad nor mom could read or write. I had the job of reading and writing for them. Musically dad was self-taught; he played the concertina and taught me to sing. To raise some money I held concerts in the back yard and charged the audience a halfpenny to hear me sing. I also sang for the lady in the cake shop in Foundry Road; she gave me some broken cakes for my trouble. I once had an invitation to sing on the Carroll Levis discovery show at the Aston Hippodrome'.

Jessie sang this song, which had a Romany tune, to her mom and dad because, as she said, 'they adored each other':

ROMANY

*Romany I see the campfires gleaming
Romany the night my heart was dreaming
Music so tender made me surrender
Lost in the gypsy love song
I'm broken hearted now that we've parted
Leaving us just a memory*

*Romany no other arms can hold you
Romany no other love enfolds you
So think of me when you are far away
And I will remember you and your love song
You were my Romany*

Lillian Turton remembers:

Like many of his contemporaries, granddad Leonard was a talented musician, and was able to play the concertina whilst others performed on the violin or sang.

Elsie, the daughter of Edward Badger (1893-1948), accompanied her uncle Maize to local pubs. Inside he played the accordion whilst Elsie entertained the customers by dancing on the pub tables. One of Edward's sons, Arthur, picked up

an accordion and started to play it straight away even though he had never had any tuition. The incident happened one day during his Second World War army service as a 'Desert Rat'. He also saw service in Sicily, Italy and Holland.

Mr Boswell is an elderly Warwickshire Romany who has travelled for over seventy years of his life. He confirmed that civil marriage ceremonies are preferred today because of the need to conform and the necessity of having legal documentation. This was not always the case as Jessie Loveridge recalls:

My Aunt Lisa, dad's sister, had to give legal evidence to get me a birth certificate because nobody bothered to register me when I was born. I needed the certificate to get married to Charlie Bamford when I was 18 years old. I now have 4 sons and 4 daughters, 26 grandchildren, 28 great-grandchildren.

Jessie Loveridge aged 17 1941 (Jessie Loveridge)

Lillian Turton's mother, Lucy Silvina Allan, née Loveridge (1895-1978) was born in a tent on the Black Patch and told Lillian that a family Bible existed with all the names of her ancestors handwritten inside it. Lucy tried to find the Bible when she was due to get her old age pension, enquiring at all the local churches; she thought it might have been left at Handsworth Old Church but it was never found. This appears to be a common way in which gypsies recorded important family events. This reflected the practices of the wider population.

However, various popular myths have surrounded early gypsy marriages, including 'jumping the broomstick or fire' and the mixing of blood. Mr Boswell recounts how the gypsy known as the 'King' of the group to non-gypsies and the 'Headman' to gypsies would perform the marriage ceremony. His version involved two chamber pots; one would be taken to the bride's tent, wagon or varda and the other to the groom's. After a short time both would appear carrying their chamber pot and hand them to the headman. After mixing the contents of both together, the headman would pour the mixture on the ground and announce: 'Only he that can separate this mixture can separate this man and woman'. At this they were declared married in the eyes of the gypsies.

Gypsy marriages between close relatives were common and some would only marry within the same name group. However, plagues that ravaged the population of England during the seventeenth century also depleted gypsy numbers, resulting in the necessity of finding partners from outside the gypsy community thus introducing new blood.

Mr Boswell explained that, after marriage, a Romany bride had to possess three bowls and five buckets. He continued by revealing that your face should never be washed in the same bowl as the one used to wash the plates. A cup or plate that developed a crack or became chipped could not be used again. If a dog licked a plate or cup they must be broken, but it was acceptable for a horse to eat from them.

Numerous gypsy traditions developed over a thousand years of nomadic travel, 'Never trust a person with a crossed eye', being just one of them.

Mystery surrounding gypsies is feared by some and respected by many. An article entitled 'Gypsy Ceremonial Purity' is an example of this. Some rituals are still being practised; others have faded away or have been overtaken by modern lifestyles.

I was talking the other day with a middle aged English Gypsy, one of the Smith family, and he said: 'I can cook anything plain as well as most women; but then, of course, I've had lots of practice, being, as I'm the father of eight children'. 'How so' I asked. And he answered 'Why, every time the old woman was chiv'd to wuddrus (brought to bed in childbirth), I had to do everything for a month afterwards, that's our way. She has her own cup and saucer and plate; and when the months up we break 'em. It's going out now, but the real old-fashioned gypsies they'd make her wear gloves even after the month was up, and, of course, she mightn't touch dough for a whole year afterwards. Journal of the Gypsy Lore Society, Vol 2, 1890/01 p 382

Another popular tradition was that following childbirth gypsy women would not go out to work because it was believed to be unlucky to do so before the child had been baptised and the mother 'churched' (a religious purification ceremony following the birth of a child).

Bereavement also had its own traditions. Following the death of a gypsy, the body would be laid out on the floor of their tent, wagon or caravan and lighted candles placed around the body. Men from the immediate family would sit with the corpse for three days and three nights.

Birmingham Gypsy Funeral c1950 (Ray Evans)

During this period no meat would be cooked or eaten on the camp. Then the body would be taken to church (either non-conformist or Church of England) followed by a burial or cremation in the same way as the non-gypsy. Following the funeral, the mourners would return to the deceased gypsy's home. Jewellery or money would be distributed amongst the women, and the men would inherit the livestock. The mourners would then gather around and observe the dwelling place being ceremonially set on fire, after which life on the camp would return to normal.

John Murphy recalls that in about 1939 he looked through a caravan window at a dead relative. Aged about ten at the time, he was later taken to see the caravan on fire near the Black Patch. To the non-gypsy it may seem to be a terrible waste to destroy a perfectly good dwelling place but Mr Boswell concluded: 'No gypsy would live in a wagon that a corpse had laid in'.

Some modern house-dwelling gypsies have carried out a modified version of these rites by placing the body in a new garden shed, with everything else performed as before and the shed and its contents burned. Christine told this story relating to her Romany roots about her great-grandmother. Her grandmother, who lived in a stone cottage in a rural village on the Derbyshire and Staffordshire border, invited her elderly mother to live with her family. After travelling all her life, it soon became evident that the old woman could not live indoors so a wooden shed was erected for her in the cottage grounds where she contentedly lived out her days with her elderly horse as company. The gypsy influence has been passed on to her great-granddaughter, Christine, who experiences prophetic dreams, only washes clothes on a Monday and uses the traditional gypsy remedy of flour mixed with water to cure diarrhoea.

Every Sunday morning, when they were old enough, two of Edward Badger's children, Fred and Sylvia, visited their paternal grandparents' house. Their gran, Elizabeth, would be waiting at the top of the entry in Hingeston Street, Brookfields, and her welcome included a quick inspection to see if they were clean and tidy. Their house contained furniture that had newspaper wrapped around the legs, so that it would not get scratched, paper covered the lino on the floor and they had a large oval boiling pot suspended over the coal fire (all gypsy traits).

Boiling in the pot were parsnips, carrots and a 'spotted dick' (suet and currant) pudding and, before they left, they were each given a portion wrapped in cloth to eat on the journey home and a penny tram fare.

In the summer of 2001 a gypsy came to the door of Mrs Mellar in Streetly who, after purchasing two embroidered tablecloths, was told to give one away and keep the other for herself. She then received a lucky twopence piece from the gypsy. Trying to find out what lay ahead Mrs Mellar asked the gypsy to tell her fortune, but astonishingly this request was declined. The gypsy, making to leave, said: 'Sorry, I have to catch the bus. In the past gypsies would normally have 'duckered' (told fortunes) when asked. The pace of modern life has now obviously caught up with them.

In the summer of 1985 Brian Wyeth visited a gypsy fortune-teller on a caravan site at Wyrley, Staffordshire and arranged a reading of his palm. He was asked whether if there was anything bad in the reading he would want to be told about it. He answered 'yes', confident that there was no way the gypsy could have any prior knowledge about him or his family. The gypsy immediately identified that he had five children and all of her other predictions came true. On his return to the caravan site two years later he found that the gypsy no longer did readings due to her Christian belief.

Pauline Taylor was a young girl living in Small Heath when she had her fortune told by a gypsy who said:

You will meet a gypsy lad with marriage to follow, give birth to three daughters and live in another country. In this new country you will unfortunately lose one of your daughters.

These predictions were eventually realised. She married David Badger, a descendant of the Black Patch gypsies, raised a family of three daughters and emigrated to Australia, where one daughter sadly died at the age of fourteen.

Two unrelated stories by women who wish to remain anonymous are included to help to illustrate the mystery surrounding gypsies. A gypsy woman knocked on a door in the Parkbrook area of Bentley one day in 1928. The woman who answered was told that a baby boy would be born to her in two and a half years' time. After the woman refused to part with her money the gypsy uttered the words: 'There will come a day when you will wish I were here to tell you a bit more' as she walked away. In two and a half years, almost to the day, a baby girl was born to the woman and, for the rest of his life, the baby's father was unwell. As this little girl grew up, every time her dad was ill she remembered her mother repeating the story, adding: 'I wish the gypsy was still here'. The girl did not help matters as she kept singing a gypsy song she had learned. She can now only remember the first two lines:

Don't you trust him gentle maiden
Though his voice below be sweet

The granddaughter of a Small Heath gypsy believes she has inherited the power of the curse. At the age of fourteen she threw a tantrum after finding out her sister had poked out the eyes of her favourite doll. During the outburst she said: 'I hope something of yours goes wrong'. Immediately a watch, the prized possession of the offender, dropped to the floor from the kitchen sink and broke open.

CHAPTER FIVE
THE CURSE ON BIRMINGHAM CITY FC

 For numerous generations female gypsies, frequently with a young child in tow, would go from door to door selling lucky white heather, trinkets and pieces of lace or offering to tell fortunes. Sometimes purchases were made out of fear that, if the household did not buy goods, a curse of some kind would be placed on it. However not all gypsies are able to issue curses. Those who have this power are only able to use it to vindicate some wrong that has been done to them or their family.

Toria, the daughter of Albert Smart, states that:

If a curse is used it should not be abused.
Curse only as a last resort to a great wrong.
Better not to curse at all, it could rebound.

Towards the end of the nineteenth century one curse was issued which seems to have remained effective until the present day. Small Heath became part of Birmingham in 1838 and derived its name from a small or narrow piece of heathland. Before this area was subsumed into Birmingham, it was predominantly rural with green fields, leafy lanes and farms. This later gave way to quarrying that catered for the housing boom that Birmingham was then experiencing. Eventually eight brickworks occupied a hundred acres of this intensively quarried area. Over preceding centuries, the gypsy would most certainly have travelled through here or even stopped to make camp on the heath. One day in 1895 two gypsy families, the Smiths and the Lees, made a stop alongside the football ground belonging to Birmingham City Football Club.

The reason that the gypsies stopped was to light a fire to heat stones intended to warm the bed of a

seriously ill gypsy child. Before the fire could heat the stones an official from the football club ordered the gypsies to move on. The child was so ill with pneumonia that the gypsies only moved a short way then stopped outside a church, probably St Andrews, and made camp for the night. During the night the child died. Soon after the gypsies sought out the official who had moved them on, believing that it was preventing them from warming the bed early enough which had led to the child's death. The official received the following curse: 'your club will never win a major competition'.

This curse has held into the twenty-first century and several attempts have been made to lift it. One such attempt in the 1980s was agreed by a local gypsy with the football club. The terms of the agreement were that, on a given night, the gypsy would park his vardo in the centre of the club's pitch. He would remain with it through the night and leave early the following morning. Essential to the lifting of the curse was that only the gypsy was allowed to be there but, during the appointed night, he observed a flash. Convinced it was someone taking a photograph he abandoned the ritual. Several Romany families tell the story of the Birmingham City FC curse but two other pieces of folklore provide slightly different intriguing tales. Tony Matthews writes in *The Encyclopaedia of Birmingham City FC*:

The area of land where St Andrew's now stands was initially a dumping ground next to a railway line. A band of gypsies lived there for quite some time and, when they were asked to move off, a curse was placed on the club and ground

An article in the *Birmingham Evening Mail* of 13 October 1982 entitled 'Bid To Lift Gypsy Curse

On Blues' states that:

Folklore says gypsies cursed the Blues when they moved from Muntz Street to their present ground displacing a gypsy encampment

The *Mail* was reporting on an attempt by the manager, Ron Saunders, to rid the club of the curse who said: 'Since I have been here we have had nothing but bad luck'. He was helped by pensioner Walter Lovell, a settled Romany, who lived in a house in Washwood Heath. Walter's powers to get rid of a curse were handed down to him over many generations and he claimed there was a lot of truth to old gypsy curses. Tony Matthews also maintains that Ron Saunders had crucifixes hung from the floodlight pylons and arranged to have the players' boots dyed red.

In spite of all of these elaborate arrangements the curse remained. Another attempt was made to lift the curse during the 1990s by the then club manager, Barry Fry. After his team had experienced a run of disastrous results he took the following action, described in his autobiography *Big Fry:*

I learned then of a gypsy curse which was said to have been put on the ground. I set about relieving St Andrews of this millstone by relieving myself –in all four corners of the pitch.

Unfortunately for Birmingham City Football Club, and Barry Fry, the curse lingered. The club's fortunes remained unchanged and Barry Fry was eventually fired.

Peterborough United
FOOTBALL CLUB
London Road - Peterborough - PE2 8AL
Telephone 01733 563947   Facsimile 01733 344140

Ted Rudge
118 Cropthorne Road
Shirley
Solihull
B90 3JJ

15th November 2001

Dear Mr Rudge

Thank you for your recent letter and your kind words about my book.

In short I was told by someone (and I cannot remember who) that if I peed in the four corners of the pitch it would remove the Gypsy's Curse which I did.

Although I am not superstitious myself when you have not won a game for three months you will do anything!

Yours sincerely

Barry Fry
Manager

THE POSH

Chairman Peter Boizot MBE DL , Vice Chairman Roger Terrell , Directors Alf Hand, Philip Sagar
Manager Barry Fry, Chief Executive Nigel Hards
Ticket Line 01733 319863, Club Shop 01733 319666, Club Information Line 09068 121654
e-mail address football@theposh.com - Official Peterborough United Website www.theposh.com
Full Members of the Football Association - Associate Members of the Football League - Registered in England No. 290803
VAT No. 120167319

Letter from Barry Fry

CHAPTER SIX
TRADITIONAL STOPPING PLACES

From the middle of the nineteenth century all gypsies were faced with more and more of their rural domain becoming part of developing conurbations and with accompanying legislation that would put more and more pressure on the English gypsy to conform. Towards the end of the nineteenth century there were travellers who required a more settled life for themselves and their families. They achieved this by forsaking the life of the road to live in a brick built house, to work in one of the many new factories and to send their children to a regular school. However many other Midland gypsies continued with their old life, maybe tradition or economic circumstances preventing more from seeking a new way of living.

The gypsy who gave the curse to St Andrew's Football Ground would most certainly have been a member of the gypsies from Staffordshire, Worcestershire or (more likely) Warwickshire who decided to continue to travel. Midland travelling gypsy families, however, faced further erosion of the places they were able to find to pitch their camp on. Land not previously considered for building was now a target for future development due to the increasing need to build more homes. Unfortunately for the travellers some of this ground was the very land on which they had previously settled without problems.

At the beginning of the twentieth century there were still many thousands of Birmingham and Midland travelling gypsies but the number of sites they frequented had started to decline. By the early 1950s most sites and gypsies had disappeared. The following sites, dating from 1900, have been identified by people who lived near them. They either befriended the gypsies or just knew they were there. Not all were gypsy

winter quarters but were places which various travelling groups regularly used as stopping places.

Willenhall was where Pat remembers the time when as a young girl gypsies with their brightly coloured caravans camped near her home in the village of Bentley. One day Pat and her dad ventured forward to speak to the occupants of one of the caravans, after the gypsy had called out to her father 'What's the time Master?' 'We were invited to have a look inside and I remember how clean it looked and smelt'.

The Gypsy Estate (Walsall)

The daughter-in-law of Jim Bates, who owned a cycle shop in Green Lane, Walsall, from 1918 to 1952, recalls the gypsies who camped on the wasteland around. They were there all the year round, living in caravans on land that was often waterlogged, alongside a large pool with rushes growing on the banks. Gypsies frequented Jim's shop to purchase paraffin for their lamps and would talk to him for long periods on all subjects. In the early 1950s the gypsies were moved on, the land drained, and a new housing estate was built and officially named the Gypsy Estate (now renamed the Beechdale Estate).

Nechells and Duddeston

In the 1930s Joyce Twamley passed Holbrooks sauce factory in the area every day on her way to Dartmouth Road School. Sitting on the steps of the factory she would see an elderly female gypsy, probably in her seventies, with long grey hair and dressed in a long black dress and a colourful blouse.

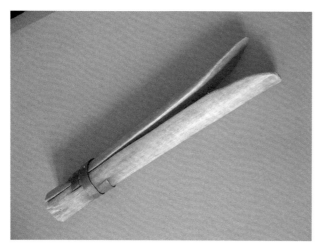

Clothes Peg made by the gypsies that once occupied the Black Patch land c1900

One day Joyce asked her mother about the gypsy and was told she was once a very beautiful woman, the daughter of wealthy non-gypsy parents by the name of Sneary. The woman was jilted on her wedding day and after this she was never the same person. Eventually she left home and joined up with a group of gypsies. She was not seen again until many years later when she appeared on the steps of the sauce factory. The last time anybody saw her was on 3 September 1939, the day the Second World War broke out. No one knew where she lived, other than 'somewhere in Nechells or Duddeston'.

Hollywood

Audrey Cope remembers the gypsy camp that she and her brother regularly visited during the ten winters preceding 1936. 'The gypsies overwintered in Hollywood's Shawhurst Lane and Houndsfield Lane. Near Simms Lane there were two ponds each side of the road near the White Swan pub. The caravans were brightly coloured greens and yellows. On the one occasion we were shown inside one, it was immaculately clean. We regularly sat around the campfire with the gypsies who would sing songs, sometimes in a strange language. The gypsy men who were always working with wood, carving and making pegs, spoke this strange language. Some of the gypsy

children went to the local school and were treated no differently than any of us. Just after the war the gypsies stopped coming when the building in the area started'.

Shard End

A new housing development during the early 1950s signalled the end of a long-established gypsy practice. Each year for a two-week period over many years gypsies would camp alongside the River Cole on land situated between Cole Hall Lane and Bucklands End Lane. Drinking water was originally obtained from pumps in the grounds of two derelict cottages, then, when the pumps were removed, it was supplied by a kind lady who lived in one of the last remaining cottages overlooking the camp.

Modern bow top varda with Billy, 2003

Kings Norton

Land adjacent to Wychall Reservoir in Kings Norton provided an ideal overwintering camp for the gypsies. It was approached via Popes Drive (now Lane) off Middleton Hall Road. Local children mixed freely with the gypsy children at play and at school. Gypsy children introduced nature to the other children, finding newts in the pond and picking pussy willow in the spring, and carved flowers and pegs from wood.

Mrs D Woodhouse, from the Heartlands Local History Society, remembers the following gypsy sites. However, she suggests that many others must have existed.

Nechells, Duddeston Mill Road

Just before the last house there was an archway that led to a yard at the side of the River Rea which was an overwinter stop for the Murphy gypsies, who may have been Irish travellers. They eventually stopped travelling and settled down in a house.

Nechells, Aston Church Road

There was a yard at the rear of houses near a bridge that crossed the River Rea. This camp used to be a permanent one. Mo Smith, a relation to the Black Patch Smiths, was the head of this group. After his death in 1948 he had a normal funeral and afterwards his caravan was burned.

Funeral of Mo Smith 1948, a relation of the Black Patch Smiths (BirminghamLives Archive)

Ward End, St. Margaret's Road, Pardoes Yard

The Pardoes, who were gypsies, are believed to have originally come to Birmingham from Worcestershire. The yard is on land that was previously part of Ward End Farm. The Pardoes were a boxing family. Tom Pardoe won a medal at the 1932 Olympic Games.

Stechford, Station Road

A fairground site that is still used by fairground people. The site was on one side of the River Cole and the caravans were parked on the other side.

Gypsy caravans rear of 24 Bullock Street c1905

Nechells, 24 Bullock Street

The house to the front resembles a converted railway carriage. In the yard to the rear were gypsy caravans.

One group of Romany Gypsies led by Esau Smith and his wife (both born in Northamptonshire) travelled the area surrounding Birmingham in the mid 1800s and eventually made their winter quarters on the borders of Warwickshire and Staffordshire. The area they overwintered in was to become known as the Black Patch.

Building at the front of 24 Bullock Street c1905

CHAPTER SEVEN
THE BLACK PATCH

No contemporary gypsy evidence exists to verify why the land now known as 'The Black Patch' was chosen by this particular band of Romany gypsies. By making this decision, they inadvertently prevented the rural location they chose from becoming an area of further urban growth. It was part of the Romany gypsy culture to settle where they would not be any trouble to the settled population. Unfortunately for them (and future generations of their families, together with others who joined them) unforeseen troubles ultimately brought the nomadic life they knew to an end. The effect the gypsies had on the local settled populace is described in the stories that are still related over one hundred years later. Contemporary newspaper reports and oral accounts passed down to current members of the original settlers' families, enable the story of the Romany Gypsies of the Black Patch to be fully told for the first time.

The Black Patch is neither a natural geographical feature nor a place name that has survived throughout Birmingham's existence. No trace of the area we now know as the Black Patch can be found on any eighteenth or nineteenth century maps. One example is the *Plan of the Parish of Birmingham* drawn by John Snape in 1779. This shows only open fields with the Birmingham to Wolverhampton canal passing nearby. Even as late as 1911 a publication by Birmingham Parks Department described the area as having been: 'One long continuous stretch of golden corn and bright, undulating pasture' forty years prior to this. This statement cannot be true, as it makes no reference to the slagheaps, which must have been there by this time.

One part of the Black Patch is in Sandwell and the other part in Birmingham. Sandwell's part is the land surrounded by Perrott Street, from the Railway Bridge along Woodburn Road, down Foundry Lane and up Kitchener Street. Birmingham's part is the garden allotments that stretch from Perrott Street to Handsworth New Road. Describing the same location in the 1850s is not so straightforward; the land was situated on the borders of Birmingham, Handsworth and Harborne, located to the far west of Birmingham Heath, south of Handsworth Heath and north of the town of Smethwick, then in the parish of Harborne. Handsworth and Harborne were both in Staffordshire whilst Birmingham lay in Warwickshire; the county boundary was provided by a natural waterway called Hockley Brook. The Black Patch developed at the point where a subsidiary stream flows into the brook on land owned by a Mrs Steward. John Kempson's map of the *Town and Parish of Birmingham* (dated 1810) shows this spot. Downstream from this point, the Hockley Brook once powered Matthew Boulton's Soho manufactory at Handsworth as it flowed along the Birmingham-Handsworth boundary. Ironically it was the same Boulton (after the creation of the Soho Foundry with James Watt in 1796) who contributed to the area being called the Black Patch. Their Soho Foundry was situated on the Smethwick side of the Black Patch land, where it was engaged in melting down scrap iron to be used in the casting process. Coal to fire the furnaces was brought in barges along the Birmingham to Wolverhampton canal, which ran at the rear of the foundry. Some of the waste that had been produced in the furnaces from the scrap iron and coal has recently been located at the Soho Foundry site in Foundry Lane, Smethwick, which is now owned by the weighing machine manufacturing firm of W.T. Avery Ltd. It was found that the waste was so strong under compaction that certain buildings had been built on top of it, using the waste as foundations.

In view of the close proximity of the Black Patch to the Soho Foundry it is possible that waste was dumped on the Black Patch land after all the available space at the foundry site had been used. Kempson's 1810 map names the owner of most of this land as M.R.Boulton Esq. Attracted by the advantages offered by proximity to the canal network from the 1770s onwards, many other heavy industries began to spring up on the Smethwick side near the Soho Foundry. As buildings spread all the way to the county boundary, only the land where the waste had been dumped remained undeveloped. The other factories would have had a similar problem of waste disposal and may well have had an agreement to dispose of their waste at the same place. When the contaminated land was levelled in 1905 upwards of 100,000 loads of clinker had to be removed. The name, the Black Patch, was therefore likely to have been derived locally from its physical appearance. This resulted from industrial tipping during the nineteenth century, and later came to be applied to this area of land on the borders of Handsworth, Smethwick and Birmingham. Several unsubstantiated reasons why the land was so named were offered by gypsies and newspapers including:

A fight on the Black Patch took place between two gypsies. One of the gypsies died from knife wounds and his blood spilled on the land, resulting in nothing being able to be grown on this land from that time forward!

The name Black Patch appears to be due to the fact that foot racing became popular, and on a level stretch some 400 yards long, coal slack was laid down to form a cinder track as a training ground.

The sight that greeted the passengers from the train windows on the elevated line that passed through the area - pillars of smoke from the various gypsy campfires would create a Black Patch in the sky.

Many other stories have been offered to explain the origin of this name and perhaps the full facts will never be known but, collectively, they were powerful enough to create the Black Patch, a name that has remained for over one hundred years.

In 1798 an Act of Parliament for the enclosure of Birmingham Heath was passed, enabling a large portion of heathland to the west to become available for building.

Today this area would be roughly from the Jewellery Quarter to Smethwick and Handsworth with Dudley Road on one side and Park Road on the other. Apart from a small hamlet called Winson Green, two large houses called Ninevah and Bellfield and a glassworks, no other buildings existed on or around Birmingham Heath. Like many other contemporary English towns, Birmingham experienced unprecedented growth during the nineteenth century. Homes were needed for over 200,000 people who arrived seeking employment in the town's expanding industries. Land shortage in the town centre led to the urbanisation of Birmingham Heath and its surrounding agricultural land. House building began and continued through the 1800s, using more and more of the land, as shown on the 1890 1st edition Ordnance Survey map.

The parliamentary and municipal boundary at the end of the newly cut Perrott Street was soon reached, and the situation was the same over the border in Handsworth, but on a lesser density. The 1890 map also shows how the Black Patch had come to be defined by two elevated railway embankments which formed part of the Birmingham, Wolverhampton & Stour Valley (1852) and the Birmingham, Wolverhampton & Dudley (1854) railways. The point at which Perrott Street goes under the latter's railway bridge and becomes Queens Head Road is the Birmingham and Handsworth boundary.

CHAPTER EIGHT
THE GYPSIES ARRIVE...

Gypsy group on the Black Patch. Holding the horse on the right is King Esau Smith 1898

Birmingham, like other manufacturing towns of the Victorian period, attracted people in search of a better life from many parts of England and abroad. Some moved to urban centres like Handsworth to live where many large houses were being built. Others, seeking manual labour, chose the town of Smethwick where large heavy engineering factories such as iron founding, casting and rolling mills could be found. This life did not appeal to everybody that settled there.

Gypsies began to settle on the borders at the Black Patch in the mid-nineteenth century. From this location they were able to take advantage of the opportunities offered by all three surrounding areas. Living a totally contrasting life to their neighbours, this group of Romany gypsies used English and Romany as their spoken language and led a nomadic lifestyle, always on the move, often having little choice in the matter.

The *Handsworth Magazine* of 1905/6 indicates that since 1860 the gypsies had been moved from Spring Hill to Bearwood, to Winson Green, to the soap works and finally to the Black Patch. They may well have been in the area for a considerable length of time before this, and part of their trail may have taken them around the Birmingham and Handsworth Heaths, possibly making their winter quarters on the Black Patch land. With urbanisation starting to consume

Birmingham Heath with the building of the Asylum in 1847 (later All Saints Hospital), the Borough Gaol in 1849 (later Winson Green Prison), and the Birmingham Workhouse in 1850, it may be no coincidence that this was the time when the gypsies started their permanent occupation of the Black Patch. They may have been anticipating a future that would provide a regular consumer market for their wares with the ever-increasing population of the three towns. Fortuitously Hamstead, an area to the north, would remain semi-rural enabling the gypsies to collect the herbs and wood essential to their way of life

made from any bits of wood or metal they could find also provided shelter from the elements. The caravan was seen as a symbol of wealth and status within the gypsy community. Photographs taken in 1898 showing the camp on the Black Patch could just as easily have illustrated the same scene forty years beforehand - there would have been only slight differences.

One person who would certainly have been familiar with this scene was F.W. Hackwood. Born in 1851, he spent all his life in and around the Black Country and west Birmingham. He was a teacher, magistrate, town councillor and a prolific author of many local history books. One,

Gypsies sitting outside their home on the Black Patch. Industrial buildings can be seen in the background 1898

Contrary to popular belief, not all the families who settled on the Black Patch lived in brightly coloured vardos. Some lived in dome-shaped tents known as bender tents. They were constructed by pushing arcs of hazel rods into the ground, and a sheet of canvas or cloth was draped over the top. Alternatively canvas or material structures with a central hole to let out the smoke from the fires were constructed. Huts

entitled *Handsworth Old and New* (1908), contains a reference to the Black Patch and its gypsies.

The first gypsy families to settle on the Black Patch were the Smiths and Claytons who, according to Hackwood, were 'typical English gypsies' or Romanies. Hackwood claims that another family, the Loveridges, were not

Romanies in the strictest sense. They followed later bringing with them Queen Henty who (according to Hackwood) 'was an acknowledged head among the wandering tribes'. However the title Queen was not actually bestowed on Sentinia (later known as Henty) until after the death of her husband on 4 March 1901. He was King Esau Smith, the undisputed leader, who administered justice within the gypsy community on the Black Patch. As such he would have been instrumental in the decision that brought the gypsies to this area. As head of the Smiths he would surely have arrived with them.

Gypsy family on the Black Patch 1898

A column, 'Gypsies of the Black Patch', appeared in the weekly newspaper the *Smethwick Telephone* on 3 September 1954. Journalist Ellery Jephcott wrote this as part of an ongoing series entitled 'Smethwick and Round About'. The article asserts: 'it was said Esau and Sentinia had eloped together when they were young' suggesting that they would have arrived together. Their five sons

and seven daughters produced 50 grandchildren and 150 great-grandchildren, the legacy of a marriage that reputedly lasted for 70 years until Esau's death. Esau, as a young man, was described in the article as: 'A remarkable figure, a splendid specimen of manhood...he looked every inch a Romany *"chal"* (lad)'. This portrait of the leader contradicts one point Jephcott made in his next article published a week later:

It was doubtful whether many or any were of true Romany blood, but their origin was unmistakable in their swarthy complexions

As can be seen here Jephcott even contradicts himself.

Hockley Brook running through the Black Patch 1898

Hackwood, on the other hand, made it clear what he thought before and after the gypsies' arrival:

Their presence in the parish was certainly in keeping with the traditions of the locality; for till the era of Boulton and Watt had transformed the appearance of the place old Handsworth Heath had been dotted with a number of miserable huts the homes of an idle beggarly people who lived a precarious life by doing as little work as possible, eking out their existence by thieving and poaching all over the countryside.

Extended bender tent on the Black Patch 1898

Jephcott's 3 September 1954 column contained further derogatory remarks about the gypsies:

The inevitable consequences of the occupation by the gypsies...In a few years its verdure had disappeared, the brook had become a receptacle for rubbish, and soon it merited the name of the Black Patch.

Unfortunately Jephcott did not explain how he came to this conclusion. He may have just echoed the sentiments of earlier writers. Despite inevitable local hostility reflected in these two writers' articles, gypsy numbers increased on the Black Patch. The Smith, Clayton and Loveridge families were joined by the Badger, Davies, Lock, Riley, King and Owen families. The Smiths settled on the Handsworth side on land that had, until recently, been Sycamore Farm, allegedly paying rent to the owner. The other families

eventually divided up the land they wanted, some living on the Smethwick side, the rest on the Birmingham part, living rent-free. The majority of marriages were made between gypsy families, but King Esau would have to consent and give his blessing to a match between one of his people and a gaujo. The size of the community grew. Large families were common, with most of the children being born under the canvas structures. Several gypsy births went unregistered, and many had to face the consequences of having no birth certificate in later life. A letter written by Beatrice Neale, who was the dispenser and secretary to a Handsworth doctor, was published in the *Birmingham Weekly Post* on 13 May 1933:

They were a clean industrious class of people who made chiefly wooden pegs, which the women would take round the neighbourhood to sell, looking very picturesque.

They frequently came to the surgery when their children were ailing, always carrying the latest baby strapped on their backs in a large shawl, to leave their hands free for the large basket of pegs.

On one occasion there was a serious case of illness, and the doctor was fetched during the night. He was led to the tent by the husband carrying a candle, and was surprised to find he had to crawl in on hands and knees, the opening being so small. The patient was removed to hospital where she made a complete recovery.

They were always grateful for any help given them and as far as their circumstances permitted lived orderly and peaceful lives.

This gives a rare contemporary first-hand account of the everyday life of a Romany Gypsy on and around the Black Patch. Conversations between descendants of gypsy families and their neighbours concerning Black Patch life appear to be the main way in which such stories were conveyed. Most of the residents of the Black Patch were illiterate and, as yet, nothing has been found that has been written down by anyone who lived on the Black Patch during this period.

Black Patch gypsies 1898

Newspaper articles and testimony by the descendants of various families help provide a picture of the daily routine of the camp. George Owen was told by his father Edward (1883-1923) that:

At night two campfires were lit, one for the men, the other for the women and children. Each night on the Black Patch there would be two circles formed around open fires, one circle of men, the other of women and children. Over the fires would be tripods, known as devils. Suspended from the devil would be a cauldron containing the food being cooked. The gypsies would talk or sing songs, accompanied by the violin or accordion, at the same time they made objects out of hawthorn wood collected earlier from Warley Woods.

This was the time when clothes pegs, besom brooms, baskets and other saleable products were made. Samuel Nathanial Smith (1861-1947) told his granddaughter, Doris Alexander, about cooking and eating hedgehogs, open campfires, living in a caravan, travelling on the open road, hop picking and farm work. Later in life Doris would witness his skills: 'Granddad was a real craftsman with his peg making'. Jessie Loveridge recalled how her father, Leonard (1870-1940), often spoke about the time he spent on the Patch, singing songs around the campfire, peg making, busking and working on Pat Collins Fair when it came to Handsworth:

A set of wheels from his caravan was kept down in our coal cellar; he must have brought them with him when they left the gypsy campsite.

Extended bender tent on the Black Patch 1898

The women would sell the articles they had made door-to-door around Handsworth, Smethwick and Birmingham. Fortune-telling and cures for various illnesses were offered on doorsteps at the same time. Any spare clothing donated was taken back to camp and shared. Ken Loveridge recollects:

Aunt Lucy took me with her selling pegs and telling peoples fortunes. Some days she took us in the pony and trap around Watson Pool (now Sandwell Valley). Their knowledge of herbs to be found in the countryside to cure illness etc was quite remarkable.

Traditional Gypsy Art (Colin Parker)

Jessie Loveridge recalls:

As a family, we used to walk together to Handsworth Wood, Hamstead and Watson Pool; Dad would collect herbs on the way. Some of the herbs were used to make herbal tea, which we were made to drink; it was not nice but did us no harm. Dad told us it gave us strength and he was right.

The men would sell wooden meat skewers to butchers and go door-to-door; pots and pans were mended or sold. Odd pieces of linoleum were also offered for sale. At other times a flat cart pulled by a horse would be taken to Bromsgrove to collect blocks of salt and the surplus sold. Bill Walker recalls one gypsy named

Ernie Smith who sold block salt on Murdock's Field in Alexandra Road, Handsworth. This is where William Murdock, credited with developing the use of coal gas for lighting and heating, built Sycamore House. This was later demolished in 1927. Murdock was in partnership with Boulton and Watt. Bill had been told that a tunnel ran from somewhere near Sycamore House to the Soho Foundry Works (now Avery's).

Irene Loveridge on the left, Dorothy Loveridge second from the right, hop picking at Suckley, Worcestershire c1940 (Loveridge family)

Horse-dealing was another way of life. King Esau was reputed to be one of the best judges of horseflesh in the country. Many local businessmen entrusted him to buy and sell horses for them. Horse-dealing, sale of handmade wares and arranged fights were regular features of several local travelling fairs. Famous fighters who fought at the fairgrounds and the Black Patch include Jonty Copson and Johnny Bull, who also fought professionally wearing gloves. Bare-knuckle fighting was a regular event on the Black Patch where there were champions at various weights who fought for large money stakes. Edward Badger passed on to his children stories that he been told by his father around the gypsy campfires. He told of one member of the family, living down south, who was the champion English bare-knuckle gypsy fighter. Hundreds of gypsies would come to watch the fights that he and others were involved in. They were arranged on the gypsy camping ground at the Black Patch, and money would pass hands on the outcome. If the Birmingham police came to try and stop the fight, the gypsies would avoid prosecution by moving to the other side of the Hockley Brook into Smethwick which was outside their jurisdiction.

Gypsy children on the Black Patch 1898

During the summer months some of the gypsy families left the Black Patch temporarily, travelling to Worcester and other rural areas where they were engaged in hop picking. This activity continued with later generations also participating. John Loveridge remembers the hop picking:

'Hop pickers only' was the cry as we got the train from Snow Hill. We spent some time in a barn on Tuckers farm at Suckley sleeping on bales of straw with the rats. Dad had a pole that he would pull the hops down with; the women would fill the cribs with them, all the chavis and chals (girls and boys) had to work (until we sneaked off). We used to have big fires and sit round singing and laughing, they were good times.

The quality of life on the Black Patch was not always ideal due to the topography of the site. Land sloped from all four directions and this, together with a brook running through, often created severe flooding. Local businessmen took pity on the families and had a large hut built for them to shelter in when under flood and to dry out their clothes. The ability to turn a problem into an advantage has always been a gypsy asset, and this is demonstrated by the very good use made of the hut by allowing the children to play in it during the week and turning it into a place of worship on Sundays. Church of England services were held in what became known as the Gypsy Chapel, where non-gypsy preachers visited to take the service. George Owen was told:

Some nights a man named Chinn who came from Bolton Road, Small Heath, arrived at the Black Patch and preached from the Bible, the congregation would sing hymns like 'Onward Christian Soldiers' etc. Another time a minister came to the Black Patch to preach was from the church in Handsworth New Road called Bishop Latimer's.

Mrs Lois M Edwards (née Pearson) remembers her mother telling her:

of the times her father accompanied Howard Wright, the son of David Pitcairn Wright, founder of Wattville Road Chapel, Handsworth, down to the Black Patch with other young men on a Sunday evening to hold a service there for the gypsies. Near the chapel was a disused 'rope walk' where another tribe of gypsies camped in tents. In a tent provided by these gypsies a service conducted by Howard Wright who became known locally as the 'Gypsies' Bishop' was also held. Recorded in the history of the chapel is the fact that the founder conducted the first service speaking from John 3 v16. Amongst the converts to Christianity was John Rainbow, a desperate fighter who fought Mazar the fighting gypsy, they met years later at the Gypsy Chapel on the Black Patch and shook hands.

No.	When and Where Died. (Col. 1.)	Name and Surname. (Col. 2.)	Sex. (Col. 3.)	Age. (Col. 4.)	Rank or Profession. (Col. 5.)	Cause of Death. (Col. 6.)	Signature, Description, and Residence of Informant. (Col. 7.)	When Registered. (Col. 8.)	Signature of Registrar. (Col. 9.)
69	Fourth March 1901 Black Patch US	Esau Smith	Male	92 years	Horse Dealer Retired	Old age Certified by D H Burn MD	E Smith Daughter in law Present at the death Black Patch Handsworth	Sixth March 1901	W H Price Registrar

Table heading: 1901. DEATHS in the Sub-District of Handsworth in the County of Stafford

Esau Smith's death certificate 1901

In 1901, at the age of 92, Esau Smith, their leader and acknowledged King of the Black Patch gypsies, died in his caravan on the Black Patch. Esau and his wife Henty both originated from Northampton where a large gypsy site existed at Weedon. On the day of the funeral a large number of gypsies gathered to kiss their dead leader as he lay in a coffin in his caravan. Children were lifted so they in turn would remember the day the King died. Thirty of the closest family members travelled in five coaches accompanying the hearse; the rest of the large gathering followed on foot in sombre dress to St Mary's (Handsworth parish church). Although the Handsworth Historical Society has detailed all legible monuments at the churchyard, there does not appear to be one for King Esau Smith or his family. It is possible there may have been a wooden one that rotted over time or was stolen for firewood. After the interment, the mourners made their way back to the Black Patch where a meeting was held at which they elected Esau's widow, Henty, as the 'Gypsy Queen' of the Black Patch. The election of this frail 92-year-old lady to take over from her husband signalled the end of the long occupation of the Black Patch. Whilst Esau was alive, it was generally understood that the gypsies had acquired legal rights to the land as squatters. Gerald Smith, a direct descendant of Esau, believed:

The deeds to the Black Patch land rightfully belong to the gypsies! They were destroyed when the King/Queen's caravan was burnt after their death.

Jane Badger was in her seventies in the 1960s and living in the family home near the Black Patch. A walk took her past the Black Patch where she met and engaged in conversation with a well-dressed man, who spoke with an American accent. During their conversation the man claimed he owned and had the deeds to the Black Patch land. Unfortunately this person was never seen or heard from again but the incident creates doubt again as to who did or does own the old gypsies' camping ground land. Some of the present descendants still believe that they own the deeds and that all the evidence was burned with Esau's caravan after his death. This claim of the deeds and caravan's fate may have become confused over the years, as Henty continued to live in the family caravan for another six years until her own death. Only then was the caravan set on fire. By 1904 the Black Patch land was increasing in value and the legal landowners required it for factory extensions. It is probable the landowners considered that, with the weakened leadership of the 300 gypsies, the timing was right to remove them from the Black Patch.

CHAPTER NINE
...AND LEAVE

'Handsworth Gypsy' a painting by Mrs Beatrice Bullock 1925
(Handsworth Historical Society)

The Black Patch gypsies' permanent occupation of the land in the sixth year of the twentieth century suddenly became a problem for the legal owners, a Mrs E.J.E.Pilkington and Messrs Tangyes Ltd. Claims by the gypsies, who thought they were entitled to its possession, may have some justification. One claim was based on having lived on the Black Patch without sight of any owner. Another claim (by the Smiths) that rent had been paid by them rather suggests the land did belong to someone other than the occupiers. Gerald Smith was told that:

The main reason the gypsies were evicted was that Lord Dartmouth wanted the Black Patch land because it was thought coal was underneath.

The legal owners did not get personally involved but employed land agents, whose job was to sell the land. However, before this was possible, they had to remove the gypsies. Several attempts were made by the agents to try to persuade them to leave the Black Patch peacefully, including offering a considerable amount of money. Who did the agents negotiate with? Was it the frail 96-year-old Queen Henty Smith who claimed to have paid rent or members of the other families who had not? Members of the Loveridge family believe as much as £500 changed hands between land agents and some gypsy residents. As the gypsies could not be persuaded to leave, an injunction was obtained at the High Court to evict them. If the court bailiff ventured on to the camping ground to serve the eviction orders, were the conditions of the eviction order explained, particularly given the fact that illiteracy was very high amongst the occupants?

Gerald Smith, talking about his father Zechariah, said:

My dad's life was hard, he never went to school, my mother taught him to read All through his life he, like his father Henry before him, was unable to read or write and often Zechariah brought papers home from work for his wife to read to him, he was able to memorise what she had related.

The writ may not have been understood or just dismissed as another piece of official paper by the gypsies. Whether the eviction order was ever served may be questioned, considering that most of the active families were away at their summer

Gerald Smith

rural work at the time the negotiations, writ and eviction took place. This leads to the assumption that events were carefully timed to coincide with the absence of most of the fit and able. Many unanswered questions still remain. Could there have been some other logical reason why most of this robust, independent, assertive group of people were not there to resist the eviction on that wet July morning?

One question that can be answered is the actual date of the eviction. In the few publications that mention the eviction the dates vary, one simply stating: 'The land was cleared of its occupants in 1904' (Briggs, *A History of Birmingham*, p 149). Jenkins in *Mind the Horse Road* p 5 suggests the 1890s. Both were clearly misleading. The event was recorded in the *Birmingham Daily Post* of 27 July 1905 therefore it establishes fairly accurately that the Romany Gypsies were first evicted from the Black Patch on 26 July 1905. The published eviction story in the *Birmingham Daily Post* is in Appendix 2. Certainly there appears to have been

some mystery surrounding the full facts that led to the repossession of the land. However, from this point forward things become a little clearer.

It must have been an impressive sight for the local residents to see the fifty Staffordshire policemen on the last leg of their march towards the Black Patch. They marched down Crocketts Road into Booth Street before turning into Anne Street, Handsworth. On the land that was soon to become the lower part of Perrott Street from the tunnel of Queens Head Road, they lined up two abreast facing the sleeping camp. Many people from local houses gathered to see the gypsies leave, some having taken a day off work to be there. Local newspapers sent reporters to write about the eviction. How did so many people know what was going on, when the gypsies appeared not to? One speculative answer may be that the authorities were only going through the motions of eviction as a face-saving measure on behalf of the gypsies. This action could have been part of the negotiated deal agreed with the landowners' agent by the gypsies 'in the know'. If the gypsies had intended to evade the authorities they could have crossed the Hockley Brook into Warwickshire (Birmingham). This would not have posed much of a problem for nomadic people. No Warwickshire police were involved in the eviction, so the encampment must have been on the Smethwick/Handsworth side in Staffordshire (Handsworth did not become part of Birmingham until 1911). Another part of the deal could well have been that, on completion of the eviction, most of the gypsy families who left the site were provided with brick built houses within sight of the Black Patch land. Others could have been offered a place to park their caravans on spare land between houses. It is probable that the very people who employed the agent responsible for the eviction order also owned the new homes that the gypsies moved into. However in the gypsy camp that morning the *Birmingham Post* reported that:

Up to nine o' clock there was no unusual stir in the encampment. Henty Smith, the 'Queen' of the colony, was sitting outside her tent talking to another elder of the tribe when a 'picket' came up with ominous tidings.

Sentinia (Henty) Smith queen of the Black Patch gypsies 1898

The next hour and a half passed peacefully until at 10.30 am a dog cart arrived carrying Mr R Heath, the High Sheriff, Captain the Hon. G.A.Anson, the Chief Constable, and Chief Superintendent Whitehurst from West Bromwich. The assembled High Sheriff's men and law enforcers from Staffordshire proceeded to take possession of the Black Patch. A few of the 50 gypsies that were in camp that morning had already left. Some of the Smiths, including the Queen, claimed they were entitled to stay because they had paid rent. Amongst the gypsies left to confront the enforcers were the Loveridges and Badgers. They mainly consisted of old men, women and children. An altercation regarding the

absence of a notice to quit and the right to stay took place between an elderly Loveridge and one of the officials. The Sheriff's men's answer was to start cutting a wire fence. More resistance from the gypsies then followed. At this point the police moved in and the protest subsided. Five arrests were made: Ada Loveridge (30), Leonard Loveridge (16), Ellen Loveridge (22), Edward Badger (33) and Elizabeth Badger (36). They were charged with throwing bricks at the police and were released on bail to attend the Handsworth Police Court on the following Friday. Neither the West Midlands nor the Staffordshire Police museums hold any records of the eviction or the outcome of the arrests.

The arrests halted any further resistance from the gypsies and, after gathering together what belongings they could, the defeated occupants of the Black Patch were seen pushing their belongings off the land in the rain. Anything left behind was removed by the Sheriff's men and dumped under the Queens Head Road railway bridge. Seven and a half hours after the eviction began it was all over. Chris Everit from Smethwick recalls that his granddad told him he owned a donkey that was used to break up the shacks that remained on the Black Patch after the gypsies were evicted.

On 16 September 1905 the following was published in the *Smethwick Telephone*:

The daughter of the so-called Black Patch Gipsy Queen, Rosanna Locke, has been admitted to the West Bromwich Workhouse at the age of sixty. Her husband died in the workhouse about a month ago. Evidently the recent eviction has not only broken up the encampment, but also brought evil times upon the former camp-dwellers.

The real queen, Henty Smith, was allowed to stay on the land and lived for another two years in her caravan on the Black Patch. She passed away on 7 January 1907 and a large number of gypsies came

1907.	DEATHS in the Sub-District of *Handsworth* in the County of *Stafford*							
	(Col. 1.)	(Col. 2.)	(Col. 3.)	(Col. 4.)	(Col. 5.)	(Col. 6.)	(Col. 7.)	(Col. 8.)	(Col. 9.)
o.	When and Where Died	Name and Surname.	Sex.	Age.	Rank or Profession.	Cause of Death.	Signature, Description, and Residence of Informant.	When Registered.	Signature of Registrar.
30	Seventh January 1907. Black Patch no.	Sentinia Smith	Female	98 years	Widow of Esau Smith Horse Dealer	Senile Decay Asthenia Certified by M. I. Wakefield m.B	+ The mark of Bertie Smith Grandson In attendance Black Patch Handsworth	Ninth January 1907	W H Pr Registra

Sentinia (Henty) Smith's death certificate 1907

to pay their respects. At the funeral the police were again involved, but this time they provided crowd control. This was necessary in order to form a pathway to the graveside, as the funeral was attended by large numbers of people who had made their way from all over the country. 'Queen' Henty was finally buried with her husband in the churchyard of Handsworth Parish Church. On the following Monday night another large crowd watched as the Black Patch was lit up following the ceremonial burning of the Queen's caravan with all her possessions. Gerald Smith recalls:

Sovereigns found in the Queen's caravan (after her death) were given to the Black Patch gypsy children. Local shopkeepers made believe they were only farthings.

Some members of the Smith and Loveridge families believe the deeds of the Black Patch land were amongst the possessions burned on that day.

CHAPTER TEN
THE PATCH RETURNS TO GREEN

With most of the gypsies now off the Black Patch land, the owners put the old camping site up for sale, initially as building land, at a price of £500 per acre. This would have effectively joined together Birmingham, Smethwick and Handsworth if this option had been pursued. The main interest in the purchase of the land however came from a society:

Under the chairmanship of Mr John Nettlefold called the Birmingham Playgrounds, Open Spaces, and Playing Fields Society, for the purpose of discovering any opportunity that might befall of preserving an open space. (History of the Corporation of Birmingham, volume IV, 1923 p 236)

One of their aims was to provide a place where people, especially children, could enjoy fresh air away from the smoky atmosphere of the industrial sprawl. Ironically, the previous occupants of the land before their enforced removal were enjoying just that sort of life. An article entitled 'Future of the Black Patch' (Appendix No3) was published in the *Birmingham Daily Mail* on Thursday 9 May 1907 and sums up the writer's anti-gypsy feeling at the time.

An option to purchase the Black Patch land was obtained. Through public support a sum of £8,285 was raised towards a total purchase price of £12,200. One of the vendors of the land, Mrs E J E Pilkington, donated £500, while Smethwick and Handsworth Councils agreed to provide a further £1,000 each. Birmingham City Corporation was then asked to complete the purchase, and to lay out and maintain the land for a new recreation ground. However, the Baths and Parks Committee, after consideration of the

request, turned it down. The main reasons given were that it would be too costly to clear the rubbish and level the land and, as the area was liable to flooding, culverting of the brook was necessary. This decision was overruled by the main council and the offer of the society was accepted on condition that no money be spent on the layout of the recreation ground until both Handsworth and Smethwick agreed to accept a proportional cost of the Hockley Brook improvement. Proportionally, the proposed recreation parkland had six acres in Handsworth, seven in Smethwick and a further seven in Birmingham. The remaining land was acquired to complete Perrott Street, widen the GWR railway and provide a large allotment site on the other side of Perrott Street.

As well as the problems of the Black Patch area's liability to flooding, the culverting and strengthening of the Hockley Brook and the clearing of the clinker-slag mounds, there was another needing to be resolved. Before any work could begin on laying out the recreation ground, Birmingham Corporation had to remove a final group of gypsies from the land. Perhaps the group in question were all Smiths who must have remained behind with Queen Henty after the 1905 eviction and continued their occupation of the Black Patch after her death. The numbers had increased with other families having returned. This was confirmed by references made by the Corporation of Birmingham Parks Department to Smiths, Davises and Loveridges being there in a publication commemorating the official opening of the Black Patch Recreation Ground in June 1911. A decision was made to evict them and this went smoothly according to the same publication where, in the section 'Peaceful Eviction of the Gipsies', there appeared the following:

In December 1908 the gypsy residents of the Black Patch were given notice that they might at any time be required to make a move, and on February 15th 1909 they made their departure.

No mention is made of the earlier eviction of 1905 when it took a High Sheriff, a Chief Constable, a Chief Superintendent and fifty policemen to evict fifty gypsies. This time Birmingham Corporation Parks Department were responsible for the order and they used considerable tact to ensure a peaceful eviction. It was claimed that the Parks Department had given the gypsies employment in helping clear the slag and provided them with wheels to put back on their caravans. These were described as 'houses on wheels' and a temporary road was made so that the caravans did not have to traverse the rough ground. The publication went on to claim that the present King, Tom Smith, who had been working with other gypsies preparing the ground:

Has so far departed from the old tradition of the royal house by going to live in a house of brick …the Loveridges had precipitated matters and had taken a house in a road adjoining the old camping ground. Souvenir of the Opening of the Black Patch Recreation Ground, Corporation of Birmingham Parks Department, June 1911

The eviction was presided over by Superintendent Monk, Sergeant Kegan and several police officers from Handsworth with a number of detectives and plain clothes officers from Birmingham also present. Some of the evicted men scowled as they made their departure, taking their homes away from the old camping ground in order to make way for the new recreation ground. Only one unusable vehicle remained which was in danger of falling apart. The gypsies' offer to burn it was rejected by officials who insisted that 'The

land must be cleared'. It was carried between two planks of wood to the street and left there. With the land now clear of the gypsy encampment, work commenced. Some of the gypsies were offered work clearing their old camping ground and laying out the allotments for the Birmingham Parks Department. This action is still talked about by the families, who claim that their ancestors helped to clear the slag and were rewarded by being evicted. Great difficulties were encountered throughout the levelling of the site, the most problematical being a large coagulated mass of clinker slag, which had been heaped to the level of Kitchener Street and sloped right down to the Smethwick boundary. The only effective way to break up this mass was to use a wedge and sledgehammer.

The Birmingham Parks Department reported that:

The work of laying out the Black Patch was carried out by the unemployed under the supervision of the Parks Superintendent. The work was commenced in January 1909 and completed in May 1910. On average 140 men per week were found employment, working in two gangs of three days each. Corporation of Birmingham Parks Department ibid

Gravel paths were laid; privet hedges lined the boundary; elms and poplar trees were planted; grass seed was sown and rolled; the Hockley Brook was straightened and a bridge was built. A children's playground was laid out at the point were the main slagheap once stood. At the Birmingham entrance a lodge was erected for the park keeper and his family, the only family now permitted to reside on the land that until recently had been occupied by so many. Lillian Butler, who was born at 118 Perrott Street in 1912, recalls her granddad, Reuben Mills, was one of

Workmen clearing the slag heap from the Black Patch 1909 (BirminghamLives Archive)

the early park keepers and lived in the new park house. He worked for the Parks Department for 44 years.

The Lord Mayor of Birmingham, Alderman Bowater, performed the opening of the Black Patch Recreation Ground on 20 June 1911.

What had once been black was now officially green.

Black Patch (Park) Recreation Ground 2001

CHAPTER ELEVEN
WHERE DID THEY GO?

By now the area was changing with Handsworth becoming a part of Birmingham in 1911. This altered the boundaries of the Black Patch leaving the larger portion in Warwickshire whilst the Smethwick section remained in Staffordshire. With the gypsy camp now gone, the former occupants of the Black Patch were dispersed throughout the surrounding neighbourhood. The gradual gypsy migration from the Black Patch had probably started just before the eviction of 1905 and may have been one of the reasons why the gypsies were able to find homes and settle so soon after their decision to become house dwellers.

Between 1905 and 1912 gypsy families occupied houses in several local streets. Certain streets were more favoured by former Black Patch residents than others. Ironically these were all within a one-mile radius of the new Black Patch Recreation Ground, with some so close that the old camping ground was always in sight. However not all the members of one family went to one particular street or indeed to any one of the three surrounding areas. They became scattered. Not all the evicted families went directly into brick built houses. Some managed to retain their caravans and relocated on spare land, often between houses. Now living a far different lifestyle from the one they had been used to their arrival must have impacted on their settled neighbours.

One day in 1916 a very young Lois Pearson was taken by her mother to see a gypsy Queen's caravan in King Street, Smethwick, and was allowed to go up the steps and peep inside. Even after many decades, the memory still remains vivid. There were plenty of pieces of shining brass and pretty china plates round the internal walls of the caravan. The Queen's name was Smith and there were several other Smith gypsies living in houses in King Street. Just around the corner, in a static caravan on land backing on to the Black Patch, lived Jonty Smith, his wife Amelia, and their three daughters - Faith, Hope and Charity.

Jonty Smith holding Dennis Murphy's hand c1930 (John Murphy)

Rene Banford was born at 126 Perrott Street in August 1915. Her mother moved into this house, which was located two houses from the Black Patch Park, when it was first built. She recalls that the Hockley Brook ran through the park and when there was heavy rain all sorts of things like dead dogs and cats got washed down to the park:

Our mom blamed the brook in the park when I contracted diphtheria and had to be taken to the fever hospital at Little Bromwich (now part of Heartlands Hospital). My childhood memories are of the days when we grew up with several gypsy children that lived in the houses locally. One family, the Badgers, occupied the house on the corner of Kitchener Street near the railway bridge in Perrott Street. We all went to Foundry Road School during the day and played in the park after.

Bill Wheeler's mother ran a shop-cum-refreshment rooms in the Black Patch Park from 1924 to 1946 and this was frequented by families and footballers. Bill, who was born in 1915, became a good boxer and fought on the same bills as a lot of the local gypsies. His parents, Mary (Polly) and Harry, were both born in 1880, and remembered the eviction of the gypsies when men on horseback chased the gypsy women and children off the land whilst the gypsy men were away. Bill always found the gypsies were clean, honest and hard-working. Two gypsy families, the Smiths and Owens, lived in the same street as his parents - Chapel Street, Handsworth.

Lillian Turton remembers her mother talking of gypsy children who lived on the Black Patch often being so hungry that they resorted to begging for food. They stood outside the gates of the Soho Foundry where workers would share their sandwiches with the gypsy children.

Elsie Hunt was born in 1907. Her mother told Elsie that, on the day the gypsies were evicted from the Black Patch, the people living in the houses nearby kept their children indoors. Her mother forbade her to go anywhere near the Black Patch warning her that 'gypsies stole children' and 'gypsy children ran around the Black Patch without wearing any shoes or stockings'. Her brother must have been allowed to go, as she said he played in the Hockley Brook before it was culverted. Elsie remembers the dark-skinned gypsy ladies calling at the door selling lace and pins and gypsy men who cut up blocks of salt from the back of a horse drawn wagon and sold it door to door. Her son, George, was born in James Turner Street in 1933 and he remembers mixing with gypsy children at school and at play, and found they were no different from any of the other children. Children were not allowed to go near the Black Patch because, according to Bill Walker's great-grandfather, the gypsies would kidnap them. Bill, born in 1908, belonged to a local Scout group that used the Black Patch Park in the early 1920s as an outdoor learning centre. The Black Patch was, for a great number of years, a place where horses were bred, trained and sold. Another Birmingham location for this activity was the Horse Fair. In the 1920s Joan Porter's father sold horses there and found the gypsies straightforward and honest.

The back garden of the house in Kitchener Street that Esther Bradshaw moved into in 1967 overlooked Black Patch Park, and gypsy families lived two doors away on either side of her. During the three years that Esther lived there she befriended an elderly gypsy lady, then in her eighties, who lived on the opposite side of the street in a large old house. Although Esther cannot recall the name of the lady who used to sit outside her house and talk to passers-by, it was probably Elizabeth Badger. She told many stories of the Black Patch and the gypsy life in the camp, including the eviction and the death of the Queen. One story Esther was told described the time that the men living on the Black Patch were 'conned' into helping to clear the slag tips from which they were eventually evicted. Another resident of Kitchener Street, Dorothy Jukes, remembers her back garden had an incline that led directly on to the Black Patch Park, and many gypsy families settled in Kitchener Street. As a young girl growing up around the Black Patch area in the 1940s, Mavis Smith said she met and played with many children from gypsy families, but they were just other kids: 'I never knew they were gypsies' she explained. Many more gypsies would have been encountered when Mavis paid a visit to her relations' grocery shop at 45 Kitchener Street, just around the corner from where she lived. Mavis's mother, Beattie, was born in 1907 and lived in Perrott Street. Before she married her husband, Samuel, from Murdock Road, she used to go dancing with May Loveridge at a church in Foundry Lane. May was a local gypsy girl whose parents originated from the Black Patch and she used to attend the church that had been built on the Black Patch land opposite Averys.

The church in Foundry Lane was called St Johns Mission Church; the Merry Hill Sunday School was held there. The church was part of St Michaels and All Angels, Crocketts Lane, Smethwick.

Another Sunday school, where upwards of a thousand children regularly attended the various meetings, was held in the mess room at Tangye's Smethwick factory. Lois Pearson lived with her parents above the Wright Evangelical chapel in Wattville Road, Handsworth and attended Tangye's Soho Sunday School. When she was older she taught in the Sunday School herself. During the week, Lois attended Wattville Road school in Handsworth where she befriended a girl called Gerty Loveridge. They came from the Black Patch but now lived in Alfred Street. Pauline Cook (née Roberts) attended Wattville Road school in 1948, when a pupil in her class was a gypsy boy named Israel Loveridge. Israel

lived in Wattville Road in a house. His friend was Charles Hickman whose parents worked on the fairgrounds. They lived in a caravan at the rear of a garage in Holyhead Road opposite Island Road.

CHAPTER TWELVE
AFTERWORD

Many descendants of the inhabitants of the Black Patch feel a strong affinity with their history and gypsy roots. Given the paucity of documentary evidence it is vital that their story is captured before it disappears without trace. Sadly, since beginning this project, five contributors have passed away, namely: Doris Alexander (née Smith), Irene Lane (née Owen), George Owen, Fred Badger and Gerald Smith.

Although the book concentrates on distinctive differences between gypsy culture and that of settled people it is worth noting that in some respects they were the same. This is particularly true during times of war. Gerald Smith recounted his ancestor's contributions to both the Boer War and the Great War as well as his and his brother's service during the Second World War.

Although the gypsies have now dispersed, however far or near they have ended up, in their minds, the area they knew as the Black Patch will always remain their Romany home.

Brumroamin brings to an end my visit into their world and culture. It has been a privilege to have made the journey and where I will hopefully stay together with the new friendships that have been forged.

Elevated railway line overlooking a typical Black Patch gypsy gathering 1898

APPENDIX 1 -
CENSUS AND ENUMERATOR BOOKS 1891

No trace of any known Black Patch gypsy families could be found in the census returns of the area for 1851, 1861, 1871 or 1881. One reason may have been due to their travelling season as censuses were usually taken in March or April when the gypsies may have been on the move. However this is unlikely because, at some stage, the Black Patch became one of the largest permanently settled camps in the country. Enumerators more likely turned a blind eye, not bothering to venture on to the camping ground. It is generally accepted by family historians attempting to trace gypsy ancestry that some gave false names and lied about the number of their offspring. Census enumerators may not have distinguished gypsies from other homeless people sleeping rough. Gypsies were suspicious of authority and often evaded the enumerators. An extract from the 1881 census taken a mile from the Black Patch illustrates this point.

The enumerator wrote alongside the address 'on waste ground between Reynolds Street and Wills Street':

Delivered this schedule to a Gypsy Tent: a gypsy woman said they did not know whether they should leave on Sunday or Monday. She said there would be 2 men, 1 boy, 1 woman, and 2 female children sleeping on Apl. 3 if they stayed. Monday morning Apl 4th I found them gone altogether, leaving no paper with anyone.

The gypsies on the Black Patch first appear in the 1891 census.

The Smiths having returned 29 people from 5 families, Claytons 19 people from 3 families, Loveridges 9 people from 2 families and one Badger, the grandson of a Clayton. Out of the 59 people identified, 40 were shown as having been born in Handsworth or Smethwick which may indicate they were born on the Black Patch. King Esau Smith gave his occupation as a Horse Dealer and lopped 10 years off both his and his wife's ages. Eleven persons gave their occupations as hawkers and seven as labourers. Higher numbers for census returns have been claimed in other publications, Jephcott writing in the 10 September 1954 edition of the *Smethwick Telephone* states:

A census shows that there were 23 families living in the encampment. There were 33 persons named Smith, 28 Loveridges, 16 Davis and 10 Claytons. Fifty-nine of the community were born upon the 'Black Patch' greatest number of persons scheduled as living in one van was eleven.

Jephcott's writings, I suspect, were copied from an article in the *Birmingham Daily Mail* dated 9 May 1907 entitled 'Future of The Black Patch' (Appendix 3). Jephcott would only have had access to the 1851 returns in 1954, because of the hundred year embargo. The exact dates of occupation or actual numbers of persons living on the Black Patch may never be fully calculated but it can be surmised from the contemporary newspaper reports of 1905 and 1907 that by the 1870s the gypsies were well established there.

ROAD	NAME			AGE	OCCUPATION	WHERE	BORN
Foundry	Reuben SMITH	head	M	45	Labourer	Leices.	Nelson
Caravan	Amelia	wife	M	40		Warks.	Sutton
	Sarah	daug	S	18		Staffs.	Handsworth
	William	son	S	16		Staffs.	Gt Barr
	Charlotte	daug	S	15		Staffs.	Smethwick
	George	son	S	13		Staffs.	Smethwick
	James	son	S	11		Warks.	Aston
	Thomas	son	S	9		Staffs.	Handsworth
	Senty	daug	S	7		Staffs	Handsworth
	Alfred	son	S	5		Warks	Birmingham
	Zachrish	son	S	3		Staffs	Handsworth
Foundry	Alfred CLAYTON	head	M	40	Navvy	Warks	Birmingham
Caravan	Lizzie	wife	M	35	Hawker	Warks	Ward End
	Lucy	daug	S	17	Hawker	Warks	Birmingham
	Leonard	son	S	16	Labourer	Staffs.	Smethwick
	Annie	daug	S	14	Hawker	Staffs.	Smethwick
	Nancy	daug	S	12	Scholar	Staffs.	Handsworth
	Lilly	daug	S	10	Scholar	Staffs	Handsworth
	Mary	daug	S	5	Scholar	Staffs.	Handsworth
	Woodfine	son	S	3		Staffs	Handsworth
	Theresa. A	daug	S	9 months		Staffs	Handsworth
Foundry	Esau Smith	head	M	72	Horse Dealer	Nth	Weedon
Caravan	Henty	wife	M	70	Hawker	Nth	Weedon
	Thomas	son	S	30	Labourer	Warks.	Leamington
Foundry	James Smith	head	M	38	Labourer	Warks	Birmingham
Caravan	Ellen	wife	M	36	Hawker	Staffs.	Tamworth
	Delenah	daug	S	8	Scholar	Staffs.	Handsworth
	Berty	son	S	7		Staffs.	Handsworth
	Matilda	daug	S	3		Staffs.	Handsworth
	Essau	son	S	2 months		Staffs.	Handsworth
Foundry	John Smith	head	M	56	Hawker	Warwick	Knighton
Caravan	Caroline	wife	M	48	Hawker	Warwick	Hatton
	Arnold	son	S	14	Hawker	Staffs.	Smethwick
	Georgina	daug	S	18	Hawker	Warwick	Bedworth
	Amy	daug	S	10	Scholar	Staffs.	Smethwick
	Angelina	daug	S	8	Scholar	Staffs.	Smethwick
	Rito	son	S	4	Scholar	Staffs.	Handsworth

Ann	Leonard Loveridge	head	M	46	Labourer	Staffs	Wolverhampton
Street	Manta	wife	M	42	Hawker	Warwick	Hatton
	Tennant	son		16		Staffs	Smethwick
	Flora	daug		13	Scholar	Staffs.	Smethwick
	Sophia	daug		11	Scholar	Staffs	Handsworth
	Ellen	daug		7	Scholar	Staffs.	Handsworth
	Frederick	son		3		Staffs.	Handsworth
Ann	John Loveridge	head	M	22	Labourer	Staffs.	Smethwick
Street	Sabinna	wife	M	20		Staffs.	Handsworth
Foundry	William Clayton	head	M	67	Hawker	Warks.	Rugby
Caravan	Tresey.A	wife	M	60		Nth	Gumest
	George Badger	gnson	S	12		Nth	Daventry
	Emily Neal	gndaug	S	2		Leic	Burbridge
Foundry Rd	Francis Clayton	head	M	44	Gen Labourer	Dby	Shordles
Caravan	Reby	son	S	22	Gen Labourer	Staffs.	Smethwick
	Sussannah	daug	S	20		Staffs.	Smethwick
	Prudence	daug	S	18		Staffs.	Smethwick
	Francis	son		16		Staffs.	Smethwick
	Amos	son		14		Staffs.	Smethwick
	Relder	daug		11		Staffs.	Smethwick
Foundry Rd	Rose.H. Smith	head	Wid	30	Hawker	Oxford	
Caravan	Sentinnah	daug	S	16		Buxton	
	William Lock	lodger		50	Hawker	Oxford	

Key

daug = Daughter, gndaug = Granddaughter, gnson = Grandson, M = Married

S = Single, Wid = Widow, Staffs.= Staffordshire, Warks = Warwickshire,

Nth = Northamptonshire, Leic = Leicestershire

(Census and Enumerator Books 1891, from microfiche RG12 (22593-) at Birmingham Central Library, Local Studies and History)

APPENDIX 2 -
BIRMINGHAM DAILY POST 27 JULY 1905

 EXCITING SCENE ON THE BLACK PATCH

The advance of civilisation may be good for the race, but it is not always welcome to the individual. While the sedentary toilers of the towns are being told that they ought to live more in the open air and nearer to nature, those who have lived the gipsy life from their youth upward are being crowded out of existence. So far as the Birmingham district is concerned Romany defended its last ditch on the Black Patch yesterday, and was driven from the field in confusion. The Handsworth gipsies are not of the purest blood nor do they display all the romantic qualities of George Borrow's heroes and heroines, yet their enforced departure from the plot of ground that has been their home for nearly forty years was not without elements of pathos.

It cannot be said that the gipsies were evicted without due notice, for the agents for the owners of the land have been trying to induce them to seek fresh fields ever since the property became eligible for building. They successfully resisted the first attempt to forcibly eject them, and they scornfully rejected a substantial sum that was offered them as an inducement to go away peaceably. The interlopers boldly asserted their claim to remain on the ground that they had been in possession for forty years, and announced their determination to fight for their rights. Six weeks ago the owners obtained an injunction in the High Court, and yesterday the majesty of the law was impressed upon the gipsies by the High Sheriff of Staffordshire and the Chief Constable of the county, who visited the locus in quo with a strong force of sheriff's officers and policemen. The two acres and a half of waste land, that is bounded by Slough Lane and Booth Street and the London and North-Western and Great Western embankments, has in the past been occupied by about forty caravans and 300 gipsies. At the present time a large proportion of the tribe are engaged in pea-picking and other occupations, which take them into the country. Consequently there were only about fifty people to be moved on and less than a score of homes to be broken up yesterday

Up to nine o'clock there was no unusual stir in the encampment. Henty Smith, the 'Queen' of the colony, who is in her 96th year, was sitting outside her tent talking to another elder of the tribe when a 'picket' came up with ominous tidings. A row of empty carts stood at the northern end of Anne Street, and fifty policemen were marching down Crockett's Road. There was a hurried council of war, which did not come to a unanimous conclusion. Some of the Smiths had made their position secure by renting the land they occupied, but the Loveridges refused to capitulate.

ACTIVE RESISTANCE.

At 10-30 a dog cart containing the High Sheriff (Mr. R. Heath), the Chief Constable (Captain the Hon. G.A. Anson), Chief Superintendent Whitehurst (West Bromwich) and Superintendent Pilliner (Handsworth). Ominous clouds had been gathering in the heavens for some time, and they discharged their moisture in a depressing drizzle just as the minions of the law commenced their unpleasant task. Halting opposite "King" Loveridge's shanty, the High Sheriff sent his representative to parley with the enemy. The gentleman with the legal document went up to the elder Loveridge, who was leaning over a wire fence of his own construction and handling a cudgel in a suggestive fashion. He was supported by a dozen determined men, excited women, and crying children."I have a writ of possession," said the officer, "and my instructions are to enter into possession of this land and clear you off". "Clear me off, eh?" shouted the old man. "Do you think I am going to leave my home after I've been here so many years? I don't. Don't you attempt it, mister, or you'll be sorry for it". The officer did not reply, but after giving the people a reasonable time in which to accept the inevitable, he called out sharply, "Bring the shears". "Don't you go for to be cutting this fence", exclaimed the King in a threatening tone. "I don't want to use no violence, but I shan't allow you to do this. I've been here long enough to claim the land. Why didn't you come before? I've had no summons. If you wanted the land that bad, why didn't you act like gentlemen and summons us? You don't frighten me, mind you". Pointing to an extensive potato patch, he asked, "Do you want that? Some of you will know about this, don't you forget. You won't have it all your own way". Before the protest was completed the wire was cut, but as soon as the gipsies saw the sheriff's men tugging at the fence they followed up their threats with deeds, the women being more aggressive than the men. They picked what missiles came nearest to their hands and hurled them at the head of the destroyers. When the Amazons of the tribe came to clutches with the minions of the law the blood began to flow. But it did not last long. The police, who had been drawn up in double column in the road, remained passive as long as there was a chance of peace being maintained but as soon as violence was used they began to arrest the aggressors.

FIVE ARRESTS.

A dark skinned youth bodily attacked a man who was bringing up a horse to assist in dragging down the fence, but when he found himself in the grip of the law he shrieked for mercy in a most harrowing manner. His mother who was also under arrest turned upon him with scorn and said "What are yer crying for? They can't hang yer for that. Why didn't yer hit 'em on the 'ead with a brick, like yer muver did?" Meanwhile the prison van, which had been waiting in the background, came up to receive its human load. There was great excitement as five shrieking, struggling prisoners were pushed into the van. Three women and two men were arrested. One of the former took a large knife from her pocket under the eyes of her captors and handed it to another woman, with instructions to "let the dogs loose". Fortunately for all concerned, this little plan was not carried out. While a shed of corrugated iron and boxwood was being demolished a stout elderly woman showed fight. She was seized by two stalwart officers and led away from the scene of strife. The woman allowed herself to be dragged a few yards from the ruins of her home and then threw herself on the ground. Neither persuasion nor force availed to move her further. Symptoms of hysteria asserted themselves. "That's no good," remarked a genial policeman "we've got no brandy here" "I don't want brandy", she replied, " I'll be quiet if you won't mesmerise me" Eventually she was handed over to the care of her friends. An old man who defended his hearth with a tar brush and a bucketful of the black adhesive liquid, was disarmed, but allowed to retain his liberty. By this time the gipsies had realised that resistance was futile and they began to gather their household goods together. It was a pathetic sight to see sullen men, bedraggled women, and weeping children pushing their caravans and driving their poultry through the rain. What property they had left behind was carted away by the sheriff's officers and deposited under a railway arch and by the side of an un-adopted road. By four o-clock all traces of the encampment had been removed, and then the spectators were driven off by the police in order that the land might be cleared in a strictly legal sense. Half an hour later the High Sheriff formally handed over the possession of the land to the agent for the owners, and then the police and officials retired from the scene of desolation. Several of the gipsies remained on the land that is rented by the Smiths.In the evening the five prisoners were bailed out. They will probably have to attend the Handsworth Police Court on Friday. Their names are: - Ada Loveridge (30), Leonard Loveridge (16), Ellen Loveridge (22), Edward Badger (35) and Elizabeth Badger (36).

FUTURE OF THE BLACK PATCH

GIPSIES CAMPING GROUND TO BE MADE A PARK

In these days of utilitarianism *[that the greatest good of the greatest number should be the sole end of public action]* no spot, however crowded with memories pleasant or otherwise, can withstand the advance of the movement, which has for its object the transformation of every open space into a playground for the public. The Black Patch, no longer the haunt and home of the gipsies, more or less unwashed, is going the way of such sites, but in this case no one will regret the fact that at length the irresponsible and undesirable nomads who infected it will be obliged to seek new fields. No place in or around the city has been more appropriately described than the Black Patch. One could by no means call the name a terminological inexactitude *(inaccuracy)*, because it is a patch, and it is very black. As everyone knows it lies between the Great Western Railway and the London and North-Western line and as might be expected from its situation, for it lies in the proximity of vast works and near the boundaries of Handsworth and Smethwick, and the city, it is not exactly a savoury spot from any point of view. Abandoned as it has been for many years past to the gipsies, notorious despoilers of nature, this excrescence *(eyesore)* has merely been magnified by the addition of unsightly wigwams, fires which never seem to be extinguished, and caravans around which, on a bright summer's day, the Romany children gambol in the dirt. Not a picturesque scene, you will say, and yet it had its attractions, for did not the Queen of the Gipsies, an old lady who died recently, hold undisputed sway there since the death of her husband, Esau Smith. The Queen's funeral obsequies *(rites)* recently were of a very gorgeous character, and her numerous prodigies *(gifted people)* attended the last rites in large numbers. They are spread about the country now, but the transformation of the Black Patch will cause the dispersal of many who preferred to remain true to the old camping ground.

The Black Patch, especially as far as its association with the gipsies is concerned, has had a very eventful and not unromantic history. Half a century ago it was part of delightful open country, for the landscape at that time had not been disfigured by unsightly factories and rows of monotonous houses devoid of all pretence to beauty or conformity with the original surroundings.

As trade grew and the city expanded, all desirable ground was soon mobilised. And the twenty acres or so, which constitute the Black Patch, remained as a sort of reminder that so much, and no more, could be spared in face of the demand for every inch of available land. For more than a generation the gipsies have had their caravans there. They belonged to the race known as 'mumpers' or hawkers, and closer contact reveals the fact that they are not of the true Romany blood. They gained a profitable and constant living by selling clothes pegs, baskets and tin goods. A good business was also done in meat skewers, which they sold to the butchers of Handsworth and Smethwick. Originally the home of the gipsies was on the Winson Green side of the brook, which separates Warwickshire from Staffordshire, but some troubles arose with the owners of the land, and they trekked over the border into the Urban District of Handsworth. If the Romanichel expected to be cordially welcomed by their new neighbours they were doomed to disappointment. The authorities at once endeavoured to make them 'move on' but without success. On one occasion the elements did what human agency had failed to accomplish. On July 12th 1889 a severe storm broke over Handsworth and the Black Country. The Black Patch was flooded, and the gipsies forced to take flight.

Twenty six years ago a mission was started among the gipsies and eventually a building was erected where every Sunday some fifty or sixty of them might be seen there listening to a sermon or joining in their favourite hymn 'There is a fountain filled with blood'. On Thursday evening there was a night class held regularly and when the chapel was not occupied it was devoted to such purposes as the drying of clothes. In a way the gypsies were faith healers and the believers in the efficiency of herbs. The late Dr. Shaw who resided at Rugby House, Holyhead Road, whenever his services were required during the nightime was invariably provided with an escort of gipsies, for the neighbourhood was not pleasant after nightfall. During the last few years the pure gipsy element abated markedly. Intermarriage with pale faces became common, and the roving instinct was almost eradicated for many of the families took to living in houses at Handsworth, and this in a real gipsy is an unforgivable offence. A census shows that there were 23 families living in the encampment. There were 33 persons named Smith, 28 Loveridges, 16 Davis and 10 Claytons. Fifty-nine of the community were born upon the 'Black Patch' greatest number of persons scheduled as living in one van was 11. Nineteen of the men described themselves as general labourers, and, strangely enough only five as hawkers, leading to the assumption that this work chiefly devolves upon the females.

The Executive Committee of the Open Air Spaces Association yesterday, Mr J.S.Nettlefold presiding, decided to raise the necessary funds for acquiring the Black Patch in order to preserve it as an open space and playground forever. It was threatened with being built upon almost immediately, and the fact caused the Association to take the step above mentioned. One portion of the land belonged to Messrs Tangye and the other to Mrs Pilkington. The owners are willing to sell, and the association have a chance of purchasing the property at considerably less cost than it would be offered to other intending purchasers and towards the amount necessary the vendors have generously promised £500 each. In addition to this it will be necessary for the association to raise £8,000. It is intended if the association is successful in raising funds for its purchase, to use part as a park, part as a playground and possibly let a portion for allotments. In the course of the next few days the association will issue an appeal containing full particulars of the proposed purchases.

APPENDIX 4 -
FAMILIES OF THE BLACK PATCH

 With the passage of time descendants of Black Patch gypsies have scattered all over the world. The following accounts are from some of these descendants who have been traced and interviewed.

The Badgers

At the time of the eviction from the Black Patch in 1905 five people were arrested. Two of these were from the Badger family.

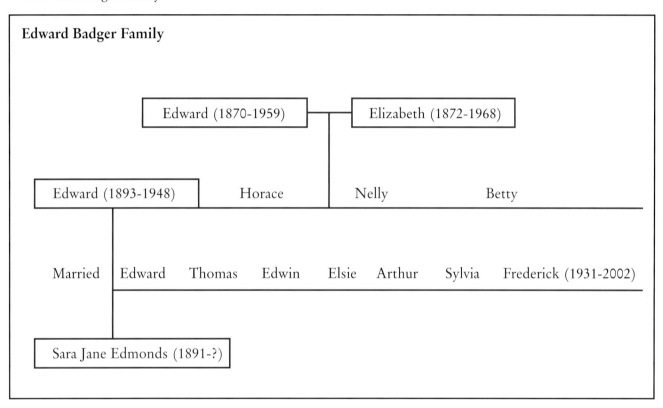

As the child, Edward, was only twelve years old at the time of the eviction he experienced both types of life, living under canvas and slates. He was living with his parents when he met the girl who later became his wife. She was Sara Jane Edmonds and, although not a gypsy, she had the appearance of one because of her dark curly hair. Sara entered a competition in a local newspaper, which offered a prize of £10 for the writer of the best gypsy story. She told of her early involvement with the gypsies and won first prize. Of their twelve children only seven survived, all educated at Slough Lane School. Edward was a master bricklayer by trade and was tragically drowned in a canal in the winter of 1948.

At the age of fourteen, David, the son of Edward's brother Edwin, started work as a slaughter man at Smithfield market in Birmingham. In the afternoon he worked in the Bull Ring market and in the

How the gipsy became her mother-in-law

MRS. JANE BADGER

The winner of the £10 prize for the best gipsy , story writes John Watt is: Mrs Jane Badger, of Perrott Street, Winson Green, birmingham. Here is her story:

When I was a girl of 16, living in Cross Street, Smethwick. I was about to go to London in service. I was just packing my clothes in an old-fashioned tin trunk when a gipsy came to the door selling pegs.

I had sixpenny-worth of pegs off her and she also asked me if I had an old dress to give her, I raked one out of the trunk and gave it to her

Fell in love

SHE told me that I would go away and come back and meet a dark young man and I would marry him. I did come home after nine months away and got a job as a barmaid at the old Vine public house in Cross Street. One night a dark man came in for a drink and we got talking. He came again and I fell in love with him.

I took him to my home and my mother said that he looked like a gipsy. Anyway, I ran away from home.

When I saw his mother I was sure I recognised her and I said :,"I am almost sure that is my dress you have got on."

She replied: "I had it given to me when I was round selling my pegs." I said: "I gave it to you. You said I would marry a dark man and it happens to be your son !"

So I do believe in gipsies! She also said that I would have a large family and, my goodness, she was right! I had 12 children, 35 grandchildren and four great-grandchildren.

Now I am a widow of 67. My mother-in-law is still alive aged 86.

Gypsy competition 1st prize winner (Arthur Badger)

evening as a doorman at a local nightclub. Eventually he met and married a gypsy girl Pauline, from Small Heath, and emigrated to Australia where he now has his own farm.

As Fred Badger grew up during the 1940s he frequently visited the Black Patch to play football on a grassless pitch. He played for various local teams before West Bromwich Albion signed him up in 1948.

Fred's sister Elsie married Billy Bagot who became the Midland Heavyweight and Army Boxing champion. One of their children, also named Billy, became a boxer, fighting on the local circuit.

The Cornicks

The Cornicks have rare documentary evidence through birth and death certificates which confirm that they lived on the Black Patch. However, there is a mystery in the family which surviving relatives would like to solve. Linda Holman is the great-granddaughter of Martha Cornick and heads the search for Martha's son, Walter, her grandfather. Linda explains:

Martha, who was a twin, came to the Birmingham area in the 1880s from Gloucestershire seeking work, probably as a domestic servant. On 8 April 1891 in the Birmingham Workhouse, Western Road, Brookfields, Martha gave birth to her first child Walter. Between this event and 1901 another child had arrived, William, born 1897. Martha, together with the two children and her unmarried partner, set up home on the Black Patch living among Romany gypsies. The story gets complicated when Martha's partner takes the assumed name of Martha's son Walter Cornick and declares himself, on the birth and death certificates, as the father of further children born on the Black Patch to Martha. Changing of his name and declaring his occupation as Chimney Sweep are both gypsy actions, but not enough evidence on their own to say he was a gypsy.

After the eviction the Cornicks moved to Wellington Street, located a few hundred yards from the Black Patch on the Birmingham side. Here another child was born and a chimney sweeping business was registered under the name Walter Cornick. In 1915 Walter Cornick (junior), aged 24, married Florence Myatt. They had two daughters, one of whom was Linda Holman's mother, Rose. Walter Cornick left his wife and young family in 1918 and since 1919 no trace can be found of Linda's grandfather either as Walter Cornick or, as he often called himself, Walter Shuttleworth Cornick. His younger daughter Amy was told that her father had joined the Mormon faith, but this has not been proven.

Keith Davis has always believed that his family came from gypsy stock. They lived for some time around the Black Patch area, where his father, Samuel (born 1907), and his siblings were brought up. He married Violet Mary Haynes (born 1911) from a farming family in Henley-in-Arden. They raised four children, Brian, Rita, Graham and Keith. Keith remembers his mother calling to her children each time they were going out: 'Don't go far' and his father always adding:

My Mother said that I never should
Play with the gypsies in the wood

Alexander Davis (Alex), no relation to Keith, was born on the Black Patch in the 1880s and lived well into his nineties. He was one of four children but his grandson, Ray, does not know his granddad's exact date of birth or his grandmother's name. They raised three daughters and three sons, one of whom, Leslie (Ray's father), was born in Avery Road, Smethwick, in 1926 where the family had moved to following the eviction.Leslie married Elsie Thornton who lived in Chapel Street and they had three sons, Leslie, Ray and Colin. When Ray's parents moved to Gibbons Road, Selly Oak, they found Fred Loveridge living next door to them. He was a descendant of the Loveridge family from the Black Patch. Many a gypsy conversation passed between the two families over the garden fence and elsewhere.

The Loveridges

Three members of the Loveridge family were arrested during the eviction in 1905. They were: Ada (born 1875), Ellen (born 1883), and Leonard (born 1889). Another Leonard, who was probably born on the Black Patch in approximately 1870, headed this branch of the Winson Green Loveridge family.

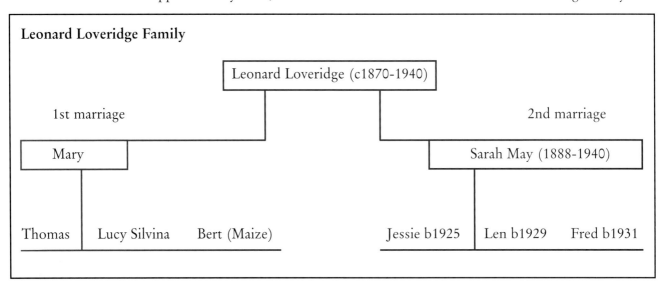

Leonard Loveridge Family

Leonard Loveridge (c1870-1940)

1st marriage   2nd marriage

Mary   Sarah May (1888-1940)

Thomas   Lucy Silvina   Bert (Maize)   Jessie b1925   Len b1929   Fred b1931

Maize's son, John Loveridge, shows great affection for his Romany roots. He is able to speak some of the Romany language and is obviously proud of his family, their achievements and how they coped with the daily struggle of life. In John's own words the origins of the Winson Green side of the Loveridge family were:

Dad was born of Romany Gypsy parents in a vardo going through Ludlow. Our family like the other gypsy families were given rented houses when they had to leave the Black Patch. We all lived up a yard 2/226 Winson Green Road opposite the prison. Next door was Uncle Tom with his wife Polly and Harold, Stan and Ronnie. Next to them lived our Granddad Len with Aunty May, Len, Fred and Jessie. Opposite was Aunty Lucy together with Jackie, Dennis, Lilly and Patricia. Looking back times were not easy like when my sister Dorothy got married at Handsworth New Road church (Bishop Latimer's), we could not go to the wedding because we had no good clothes. One Christmas Les had a cowboy hat, I had the belt and Donald the gun and that was it. Our family left Winson Green in 1947 to live in Latelow Road, Lea Hall (Kitts Green)

Leonard Loveridge 1870-1940 in Boer War uniform 1890s
(Lilian Turton)

Another of Maize's sons, Kenneth (Ken), added further memories :

The Romanies all lived in caravans on Black Patch Park which was then common land. When granny Loveridge (Mary) died the caravan etc was burnt. Fruit, potatoes, and hop picking was an annual thing to do. Ferrets and dogs were used for hunting, trapping rats and rabbits etc, maggots from farms for fishing. When the eldest of the family died everything was burned, that was the way of the Romanies.

Tom Loveridge 1950s (Ron Loveridge)

Ivy Taylor, one of Maize's daughters, remembers her granddad Leonard very well:

Granddad always wore a dickey bow, corduroy jacket and trousers with kneepads. With his black hair plastered back that included a wave on the fringe, granddad used to sit on the fireguard in the house and play his concertina.

Leonard's other son, Thomas, together with his wife, Mary, and their three sons left Winson Green in 1940. They loaded their goods onto a horse and dray that had hoops of willow fitted from side to side with a canvas sheet draped over the top. The family settled in the back and set off towards Worcester in search of a rural location. Their son, Stan, remembers having to sleep in a field at night and, when they encountered hills, having to help the horse pull the load. On arrival at Stocks Farm in Suckley, after travelling for four or five days, the family lived in the hop barracks on the farm. Eventually they settled in Bridgehouse Cottage.

Stan's younger brother, Ron, recalls having a horse called Turpin, catching rabbits for the family to eat and obtaining chickens and eggs from the farm. They also picked hops and fruit and trapped moles for

Ron Loveridge with Turpin, Hop picking 1940s (Ron Loveridge)

the farmer. Ron, in later life, retained his love of the countryside and is at present a Water Bailiff with the Droitwich canal and River Salwarpe.

Tennant Loveridge (1875-1943) was born on the Black Patch and is buried with his wife Sarah (Ann) in Handsworth Cemetery. Tennant had two sisters (both probably born on the Black Patch), one of whom lived in Booth Street, Handsworth, and the other on the corner of Avery Road, Smethwick.

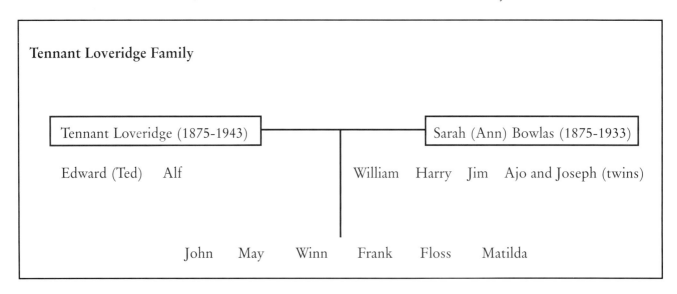

Tennant Loveridge Family

Tennant Loveridge (1875-1943)   Sarah (Ann) Bowlas (1875-1933)

Edward (Ted)   Alf   William   Harry   Jim   Ajo and Joseph (twins)

John   May   Winn   Frank   Floss   Matilda

His granddaughter, Winifred, believes that Tennant was the old gypsy Queen's son but, for this to be true, a change of name from Smith to Loveridge would have needed to have taken place, (unless there were two queens, one for each group). The family caravan, in which some of their thirteen children were born, was pitched on the Woodburn Road side of the Black Patch land until the eviction. The first three children were born on the Black Patch whilst it is probable the others were born in the house in Foundry Lane, Smethwick, which Tennant and Sarah occupied following their eviction. Later the family resided at 27 Avery Road, Smethwick, and from both of these addresses they could still see the land that Winifred claims her granddad once owned but lost the deeds to the Black Patch.

Tennant and some of his sons were bricklayers and helped to build the Smethwick Council House, a new part of the prison in Winson Green, and the walls of the Hockley Brook, which ran through the Black Patch. Winifred's father, William (1903-1953), married Frances Beatrice Horton who was not a gypsy.

Joseph Loveridge, the surviving twin c1920 (Ted Loveridge)

The Soho Foundry, just across Foundry Lane from the Black Patch, was the location where Tennant's sister first told Winifred about the spiritual happenings outside the gates. Several people, including members of the Loveridge family, have experienced the presence of what became known as the 'Grey Lady'. A man and his wife experienced the first sighting of the apparition at midnight. Tennant's wife, some time later, also had a sighting but she thought it may have been the Queen of the gypsies. Another claim relating to the 'Grey Lady' is that she lived in one of the cottages just inside the main gates of Soho Foundry. Her name was Pat Collings, a cleaner, whose husband also worked at the foundry as a train driver. He was killed in an accident. Pat was carrying two pails when she was told of his death. She let out a piercing scream and dropped the pails then collapsed dead. It is believed the 'Grey Lady' wanders around looking for her husband.

Ted Loveridge is the son of one of the twin boys born to Tennant and Sarah. Although he is of Romany stock, his father was not brought up in the Loveridge family:

The twins Joseph and Ajo were born on 11 February 1910. Ajo did not live very long. His death resulted in Joseph being separated from the rest of the family. Information passed down through the family to Joseph's son, Edward (Ted), states that Romany superstition decrees: 'If one twin dies the survivor must leave the family'. Joseph went to live with a Mrs Lillian Bowker in Middlemore Road. Lillian brought Joseph up as one of her own, alongside her family.

The Owens

The Owen family are linked directly to the King and Queen of the Black Patch by Emma Owen's marriage to Samuel Nathanial Smith. Somehow the young son apparently left behind by Emma at Aston eventually found his way to the gypsy Black Patch camp. He was probably brought up there by either his mother and stepfather, Emma and Samuel, or by another family. The name of the young boy was Edward Owen. He was born in 1883 and died on 6 December 1923, aged 40, as a result of rheumatic fever contracted through sleeping rough on the Black Patch.

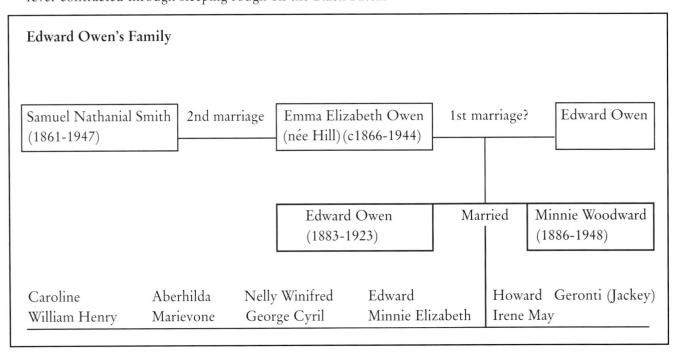

Edward Owen's Family

Samuel Nathanial Smith (1861-1947)	2nd marriage	Emma Elizabeth Owen (née Hill) (c1866-1944)	1st marriage?	Edward Owen

	Edward Owen (1883-1923)	Married	Minnie Woodward (1886-1948)

Caroline William Henry	Aberhilda Marievone	Nelly Winifred George Cyril	Edward Minnie Elizabeth	Howard Geronti (Jackey) Irene May

Minnie Owen, George Cyril's wife (Irene Lane)

Aberhilda Owen age 96 born on the Black Patch Oct 1904

Minne Elizabeth Owen aged 80

Edward's youngest daughter, Irene May, born on 16 June 1923 (the same year that Edward died), explains:

Mom and Dad were blessed with eleven children. The first two, Caroline in 1905 and Aberhilda in 1904, were both born on the Black Patch. The others were either born in Perrott Street, Winson Green, where the family first went to live after leaving the Black Patch or at 11 Woodbine Terrace, Chapel St, Handsworth, where they subsequently moved to. None of our family knew our proper granddad. I was always told he was called Edward and he went to prison, where eventually he died. Living in the same street as us was our grandmother, Emma and step-granddad, Nathanial. I remember him as a kind proud gypsy man. He would walk upright down the middle of the road in Booth Street. One day, when I was 24, he died in hospital following an accident with a horse and cart in Handsworth'.

Irene's brother, George Cyril Owen, was born in 1919. However, his daughter, Linda, has never fully known the family story. George, who was in his eighty-first year, recalls hearing

The area around Black Patch had got the reputation among the gypsies of being a good site for hawking etc around the local houses. Dad's two eldest daughters were both born under the canvas on the Black Patch. Caroline the eldest, never had a birth certificate and Aberhilda was the other sister.

Cornelius Scarrat moved his caravan off the Black Patch camping ground and set up his home in an opening in Gladys Road, Smethwick near to number 42. He lived a gypsy life from this location until his death in 1936, after which the caravan received the traditional gypsy treatment and was ceremonially burned.

The Smiths

Horatio Smith was born on the Black Patch in approximately1865, but the name of his wife or the size of their family is not known. Lynn Shortt, his great-granddaughter, was told that the family was the first to leave the Black Patch and live in a house. They moved to Bacchus Road, Winson Green. One of Horatio's children, Elizabeth (born in 1891 on the Black Patch), married Sid Brooks and they brought up thirteen children in Talbot Street, Winson Green. The house was so small that when all the family were together they would eat off plates held in their hands, seated on the stairs. Horatio, sporting a prominent handlebar moustache, would cycle from the Stratford area to visit his daughter and her family until sometime in the 1930s.

Gerald Smith, the great-grandson of Esau and Sentina (Henty), produced this account of his family.

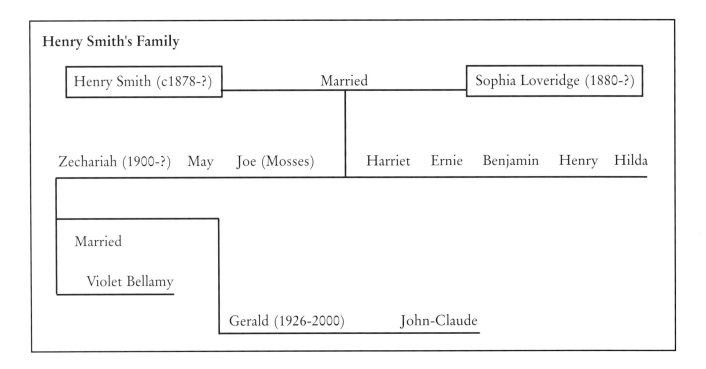

Henry Smith's Family

Henry Smith (c1878-?)   Married   Sophia Loveridge (1880-?)

Zechariah (1900-?)   May   Joe (Mosses)   Harriet   Ernie   Benjamin   Henry   Hilda

Married

Violet Bellamy

Gerald (1926-2000)   John-Claude

Sophia was probably Leonard Loveridge's sister and moved off the Black Patch at the same time as the other Loveridges to live at the rear of 226 Winson Green Road.

Gerald remembered being told by his father:

Tangye the factory owner picked the queen up and took her for a ride in his horse and trap. George Tangye, who was on the bench, and always evinced an interest in the gypsies, drove her back to her home in his carriage.

Employment was a problem for Gerald resulting in a variety of jobs because of his inability to settle whenever there was a roof over his head, and his desire for fresh air. Plenty of this was found on his final job with the GPO (now British Telecom) for whom he worked for thirty six years until retirement. Ironically he was based just a few hundred yards away from the Black Patch in Booth Street, Handsworth.

Samuel Nathaniel Smith, son of Esau and Henty, told their granddaughter, Doris Alexander, about their days as Romany gypsies living on the Black Patch.

Henry Smith one of the sons born to Esau and Henty c1900
(Gerald Smith)

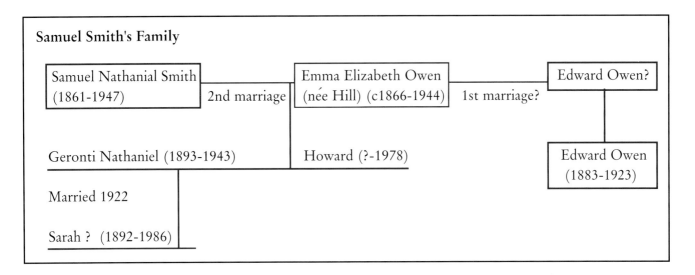

Samuel Smith's Family

| Samuel Nathanial Smith (1861-1947) | 2nd marriage | Emma Elizabeth Owen (née Hill) (c1866-1944) | 1st marriage? | Edward Owen? |

Geronti Nathaniel (1893-1943)   Howard (?-1978)   Edward Owen (1883-1923)

Married 1922

Sarah ? (1892-1986)

Doris recounts:

*Granddad earned his living as a horse dealer.
Along with the rest of his clan he travelled to
horse fairs, hiring himself out for odd jobs as they
travelled throughout the summer season. While
attending a horse fair in Aston, the Onion Fair,
Samuel met Emma Owen. Emma, who lived
locally with her family, was the daughter of a lay
preacher who preached in a nearby Chapel. At
the end of the week Emma and Samuel had
become close friends and when the fair moved
on she left her family and a young baby son and
travelled on with the gypsies.*

As time went on, Emma gave birth to a
number of children. The first to survive was
born on the Black Patch on 29 February 1893.
He was Doris's father, Geronti. After leaving
the Black Patch, they lived in a small house in
Chapel Street, Handsworth, where another
son Howard, nicknamed 'the black one', was
born. His birth was not officially registered.
A further move was made to number 55

Samuel Nathanial Smith standing (Doris Alexander)

opposite the old house in the same street. Her mother, Sarah, and father lived here with her
grandparents after they were married in 1922:

*During the evenings my grandparents would sit talking of the old days (egged on by me), I was always
fascinated by the stories of the Romany days on the Black Patch. He was a hard-working man, very quiet
and unassuming person. He would sit cross-legged on the floor of his shed in Chapel Street making pegs,
customers would come to the door asking to buy them. He loved most animals especially horses, it was quite
ironic that he died because of a horse.*

In March 1947 Samuel, now in his eighty-fifth year, was walking past a horse that was in the shafts of a bakers cart in Albert Road, Handsworth, when the horse reared up and Samuel was hit on the head. It was thought the horse reacted this way because of the reflection the sun made on a manhole cover and frightened the horse. Unfortunately the blow proved fatal. I have a feeling that was the way granddad would have wanted to die with the horses that he loved so much! My grandmother had passed away three years earlier in the January of 1944 aged seventy eight. Maybe they did not have much in material things, but in a lot of ways I think they were richer than we are today.

Thomas Smith was another son of Esau and Henty. His family has been traced by Mary, the widow of his great-grandson, Bert Esau Smith.

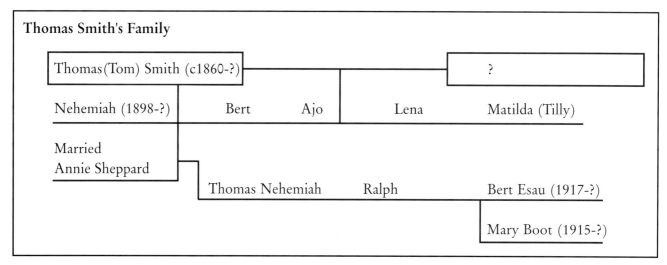

Thomas Smith's Family

Thomas(Tom) Smith (c1860-?)			?	
Nehemiah (1898-?)	Bert	Ajo	Lena	Matilda (Tilly)
Married Annie Sheppard				
	Thomas Nehemiah	Ralph		Bert Esau (1917-?)
				Mary Boot (1915-?)

Mary says: 'Nehemiah was born on the Black Patch in January 1898, his father was called Thomas (Tom)'. King Esau and Henty Smith in the 1891 census had a son living with them who had been born in Leamington. His name was Thomas, aged thirty.

Nehemiah's mother's maiden name is not known. The other members of this Romany gypsy family were, most probably, born on the Black Patch. The Smith children attended Slough Lane School and, when Nehemiah left, he was able to read and write. He lived at 3 Avery Road, Smethwick, in the house the family moved to directly from the Black Patch. With his wife, Annie, who was not a gypsy, they raised three sons. One, Thomas Nehemiah, rented a bungalow on the Smethwick part of the Black Patch, near the corner of Foundry Lane and Woodbourne Road. It is thought by many gypsy families that this was the spot where Queen Henty had been allowed to remain after the eviction until death. Bert and Mary raised their family of three children, Pauline, Avril and John, in the same house in Preston Road, Winson Green, where Mary had been born in 1915.

Nehemiah Smith standing with his cousin a Loveridge 1920 (Mary Boot)

BIBLIOGRAPHY

PUBLICATIONS

Borrow, G.   (1924) *Romano Lavo-Lil: Word Book of the Romany or English Gypsy Language.* London. John Murry.

Briggs, A.   (1952) *History of Birmingham Vol 11.* Oxford. Oxford University Press.

Chinn, C.   (1999) *One Thousand Years of Brum.* Birmingham. Birmingham Evening Mail. 0953431649

Davies, J.   (1999) *Tales of the Old Gypsies.* Newton Abbot.Butler and Tanner. 0715307029

Drake, P.   (1998) *Handsworth, Hockley and Handsworth Wood.* Wiltshire. Tempus. 0752415514

Floate, S.S.   (1999) *My Ancestors were Gypsies.* London. Society of Genealogists. 1859514014

Hackwood, F.W.   (1896) *Some Records of Smethwick.*(reprint 2001). Studley. Brewin Books. 1858581834

Hackwood. F.W.   (1908) *Handsworth: Old & New.* (reprint 2001). Studley. Brewin Books. 1858581893

Hitches, M.W.   (1991) *Man and Action.* Bath. Book Craft. 0951750801

Jenkins, G.   (1999) *Mind the Horse Road.* Studley. Brewin Books. 1858581591

Kenrick, D.(ed)   (1999) *In the shadow of the Swastika: The Gypsies During the Second World War.* Bristol. J.W. Arrowsmith. 0900458852

Okely, J.   (1993) *The Traveller-Gypsies.* Cambridge. Cambridge University Press. 0521288703

Smith, G.   (1997) *Winson Green My World.* Studley. Brewin Books. 1858581087

Stephens, W.B   (1964) *History of the County of Warwick Vol. (VII).* London. Oxford University Press and University of London.

Stockin, J.   (2000) *On the Cobbles: The Life of a Bare-Knuckle Gypsy Warrior.* London. Mainstream. 1840183845

Upton, C.   (1993) *A History of Birmingham.* Sussex. Phillimore. 0850338700

Vesey-Fitzgerald, B. (1973) *Gypsies of Britain.* Newton Abbot. David and Charles. 0715360639

Vince, C.A.   (1923) *History of the Corporation of Birmingham Vol.IV*

Ward-Jackson, C.H. (1972) *The English Gypsy Caravan.* Newton Abbot. David and Charles. 0715356801

Williams, N.   (1996) *Midland Fairground Families.* Wolverhampton. Ultra Press. 1898528047

Yoors, J.   (1967) *The Gypsies.* London. George Allen and Unwin.

COLLECTIONS

Chinn, C. Collection of letters and photographs from gypsy relatives in response to newspaper and radio articles from Dr Carl Chinn, Birmingham Community Historian, entitled "Romanies" Archive file no. 41/35, Birmingham Central Library, Archives

Hackwood, F.W. (1907 to1923)Newspaper cuttings from the Handsworth Herald. Birmingham Central Library, Local Studies and History.

Holloway, F. (1900) Collection of gypsy families photographed living on the Black Patch. Warwickshire Photographic Survey. Birmingham Central Library, Local Studies and History.

Jephcott, E. (1954) Collection of newspaper articles from the Smethwick Telephone, Smethwick Library entitled 'The Jephcott Collection'

OTHER PUBLICATIONS

Birmingham Parks Dept.   (1911) *Souvenir of the Opening of the Black Patch Recreation Ground.*
Birmingham Central Library, Local Studies and History.

Hinsley, A.   *Gypsies.* Family History (August 1999). Birmingham Central
Library, Local Studies and History.

Journal of the Gypsy Lore Society (old and new series). Birmingham Central Library, Local Studies
and History.

MAPS

John Kempson's Map of the Town and Parish of Birmingham 1810. Birmingham Central Library, Local
Studies and History.

John Snape's Plan of the Parish of Birmingham 1779. Birmingham Central Library, Local Studies and
History.

Ordnance Survey. 1st edition. Birmingham. (1884-1890). 1:2500. 25". Birmingham Central Library,
Local Studies and History.

WEBSITES

http://sca.lib.liv.ac.uk/collections/gypsy/intro.htm
Gypsy Collections at the University of Liverpool

http://website.lineone.net/~rtfhs
Romany & Traveller Family History Society

www.winsongreentobrookfields.co.uk
Local site with some coverage of the Black Patch and environs

www.groundswelluk.net/~fft/index.htm
Local site with some coverage of the Black Patch and environs

www.romani.org
International site covering Roma history and culture

Markings left on gateposts, walls, pavements, trees and lampposts in chalk. Sometimes these were in stones or twigs on paths or hedgerows.

WARNING / KEEP AWAY.	OWNER MAY BE VIOLENT.	"TEETH" FIERCE DOG. MAY BE UNLEASHED.	WORTH A VISIT.
"SPADES" FOOD GIVEN IN RETURN FOR WORK	MONEY SOMETIMES GIVEN.	MONEY ALWAYS GIVEN.	SOFT WOMAN LIVES HERE.
"A HAT" A KIND MAN LIVES HERE.	"STOOL WITH TWO EYES." SAFE CAMPING SITE	"OPEN EYE" POLICE WATCH ALL TRAVELLERS.	"CLOSED EYE" POLICE DONT BOTHER TRAVELLERS.
POLICE MAY BE CALLED.	OCCUPANT(S) HERE AFRAID OR NERVOUS.	NOT WORTH CALLING HERE.	"A LOAF" BREAD ONLY GIVEN.
OWNER IS BAD TEMPERED	IT PAYS TO TELL A HARD LUCK TALE	IT PAYS TO FEIGN ILLNESS	"A CUP" DRINK ONLY GIVEN